# Reading
## Workbook B

Siegfried Engelmann
Susie Andrist
Tina Wells

**Acknowledgments**

The authors are extremely grateful to Tina Wells for keeping the ship afloat on this project, and to Patricia McFadden, Margie Mayo, and Chris Gladfelter for their great attention to detail.

**PHOTO CREDITS**

**4** H. Peter/Alamy; **7** (tl)McGraw-Hill Education, (tr)©William Ryall, (bl)Ingram Publishing/SuperStock, (br)Andres Rodriguez/123RF; **10** (l)©Lars Christensen/Alamy, (c)©Ingram Publishing/Alamy, (r)Purestock/SuperStock; **17** (l to r)©Greg Kuchik/Getty Images, (2,3)McGraw-Hill Education, (4)lynx/iconotec.com/Glow Images, (5)Photographer's Choice/Getty Images, (6)©Ingram Publishing/Alamy; **21** (airplane)Fancy Collection/SuperStock, (cloud)Natural Selection John Bracchi/Design Pics; **25** (l)©IT Stock Free/Alamy, (c)G.K. & Vikki Hart/Getty Images, (r)©IT Stock Free/Alamy. **Mastery Tests: T-4 82** (tl)©Steve Hamblin/Alamy Stock Photo, (tc)Dieter Heinemann/Alamy Stock Photo, (tr)Ingram Publishing, (cl)©Image Source, (bl)Life On White/Getty Images, (bc)Comstock Images/Alamy Stock Photo, (br)Eric Isselee/123RF; **84** (tl,bl)McGraw-Hill Education, (tr)Len Green/123RF, (br)Comstock/Alamy Stock Photo; **T-6 98** Graeme Pitman; **99** (l)tomprout/E+/Getty Images, (r)Erik Lam/123RF.

## mheducation.com/prek-12

Copyright © 2021 McGraw-Hill Education

All rights reserved. No part of this publication may be reproduced or distributed in any form or by any means, or stored in a database or retrieval system, without the prior written consent of McGraw-Hill Education, including, but not limited to, network storage or transmission, or broadcast for distance learning.

Permission is granted to reproduce the material contained on pages 81–105 on the condition that such material be reproduced only for classroom use; be provided to students, teachers, or families without charge; and be used solely in conjunction with *Reading Mastery Transformations*.

Send all inquiries to:
McGraw-Hill Education
8787 Orion Place
Columbus, OH 43240

ISBN: 978-0-07-905425-8
MHID: 0-07-905425-0

Printed in the United States of America.

3 4 5 6 7 8 9 10 QSX 26 25 24 23 22

Name _____

# 36

## A  INFORMATION ITEMS

1. When something tries to move in one direction, something else tries to move _____ .

2. Which arrow shows the direction the air will leave the balloon?
   _____

3. Which arrow shows the direction the balloon will move?
   _____

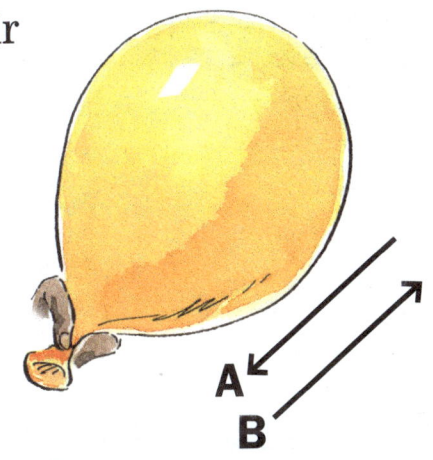

4. Which arrow shows the direction the canoe is moving?
   _____

5. Which arrow shows the direction the paddle is moving in the water? _____

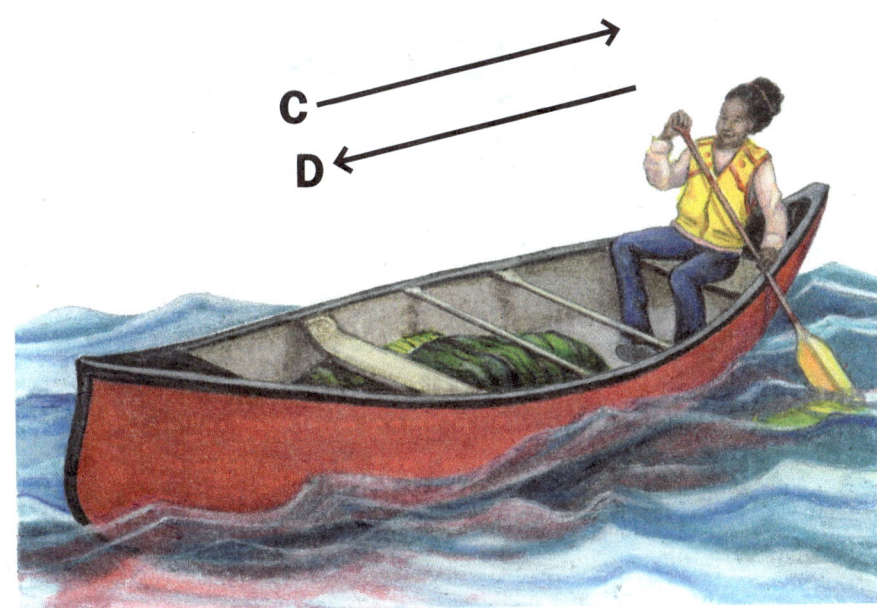

Lesson 36

The picture shows Goad filled up with air.

6. Which arrow shows the direction the air will leave Goad? _____

7. Which arrow shows the direction Goad will move? _____

8. The arrow shows which direction the boy will jump. **Make an arrow** on the block of ice to show which direction it will move.

2  Lesson 36

9. The arrow shows which direction the girl will jump.
   **Make an arrow** on the back of the boat to show which way the boat will move.

## B  SKILL ITEMS

Fill in each blank with a word from the box.

| decision | traffic | airplane | perfect | per |
| sleeping | supposed | forward | couple | |

1. The _____ was moving forty miles _____ hour.

2. He is _____ to make a _____ in a _____ of days.

**GO TO PART D IN YOUR TEXTBOOK**

Lesson 36

# 37

**Name** _____

## A INFORMATION ITEMS

1. When something tries to move in one direction, something else tries to move _____ .

2. Which arrow shows the direction the air will leave the jet engines? ___

3. Which arrow shows the direction the jet will move? ___

4. Which arrow shows the direction the canoe is moving? ___

5. Which arrow shows the direction the paddle is moving in the water? ___

6. If the paddle of a canoe is moving east through the water, in which direction is the boat moving? _____

7. Which arrow shows the direction the air will leave the balloon? ___

8. Which arrow shows the direction the balloon will move? ___

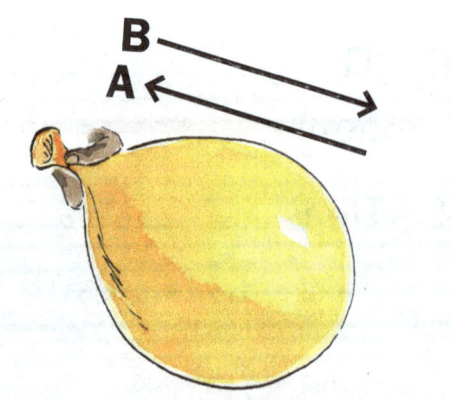

4    Lesson 37

The picture shows Goad filled up with air.

9. Which arrow shows the direction the air will leave Goad? ___

10. Which arrow shows the direction Goad will move? ___

11. When a boy jumps from the mud this way ↖, the mud tries to move which way? _____

## B  SKILL ITEMS

1. Write one way that tells how both objects are the same.
   _____

2. Write 2 ways that tell how object A is different from object B.
   ① _____
   ② _____

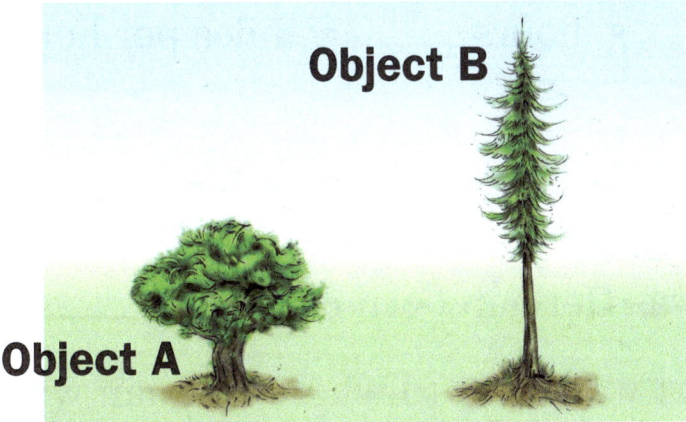

**GO TO PART D IN YOUR TEXTBOOK**

Lesson 37  5

# 38  Name _____

## A  INFORMATION ITEMS

1. What part of a car tells how fast the car is moving?

   • the tires    • the speedometer    • the clock

Each speedometer in the picture shows how fast the car is moving.

A

Miles per hour

B

Miles per hour

2. How fast is car A going? _____

3. How fast is car B going? _____

4. Which car is going faster? _____

5. A speedometer tells about ▭ .

   • miles    • hours    • miles per hour

## B  STORY ITEMS

1. What city was Herman born in? _____

2. What airport was close to where Herman was born?
   _____

3. How far was the airport from where Herman was born?
   _____

6  Lesson 38

4. Why didn't Herman fly off the cab?
   - Flies don't fly in the morning.
   - Flies don't take off near airports.
   - Flies don't take off in big winds.

5. How many legs does Herman have? _____

6. The two women were part of the crew of a
   _____.

7. Herman went into the woman's purse ▨ .
   - to stay warm
   - to chew gum
   - to eat candy

8. Circle 2 things that Herman liked about the cab.
   - It was warm.
   - It was new.
   - It was fast.
   - It was green.
   - It was yellow.

9. When was the wind blowing fastest on Herman?
   - when the cab was standing still
   - when the cab was going 35 miles per hour
   - when the cab was going 15 miles per hour

Look at the pictures.

10. **Underline** the thing that Herman rode on to the airport.

11. **Make an X** on the thing the two women work on.

GO TO PART D IN YOUR TEXTBOOK

Lesson 38

# 39 Name _____

## A  INFORMATION ITEMS

Look at the picture of the inside of a jet.

1. There are 3 flight attendants on the plane. **Make a box** around each flight attendant.

2. **Cross out** the captain.

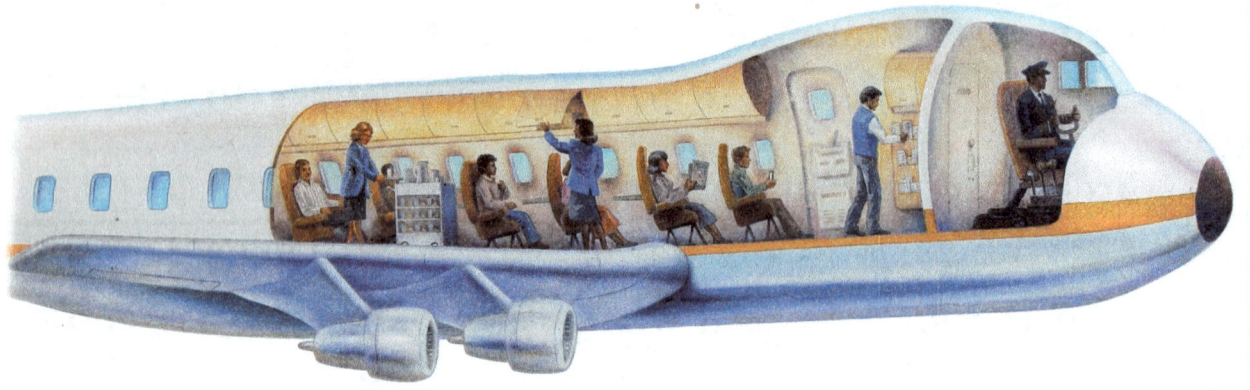

## B  STORY ITEMS

1. Why did Herman fly into the woman's purse?
   - to get warm
   - to get candy
   - to find a dark place

2. Why did it get dark inside the purse?
   - The woman closed the purse.
   - The sun went down.
   - The woman went into a dark place.

3. Herman tried to take a nap on something. What was it?
   - a wall
   - a window
   - a seat

4. Why did that place feel great to Herman?
   - It was big.
   - It was warm.
   - It was cold.

5. How far is it from New York City to San Francisco?
   _____

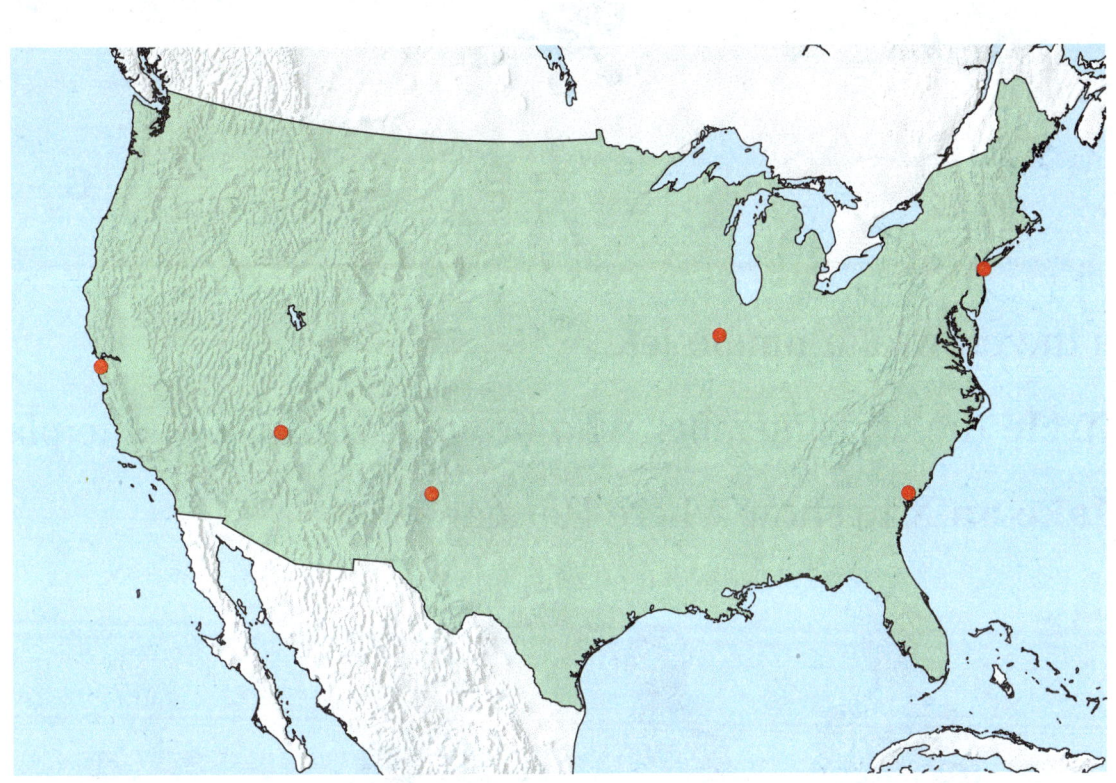

6. Make an **X** where New York City is.

7. Make a **Y** where San Francisco is.

8. **Underline** the plane that Herman was in.

A  B  C

Here's the crew of a jumbo jet.

9. **Circle** the crew member who brought Herman on the plane.

10. **Make an X** to show where Herman was.

A  B  C  D

GO TO PART D IN YOUR TEXTBOOK

Lesson 39

Name _____  40

### A  SETTING, CHARACTERS, PLOT

Answer these questions about the story *Pop's Truck*.

1. What is the main setting for this story? _____

2. Name the main characters in this story.
   _____

3. *Pop's Truck* shows how some old things can be ▆▆▆ .
   - thrown away
   - put to good use
   - sold

### B  STORY ITEMS

1. Where did Pop live? _____

2. Name 3 things the children did with Pop. _____
   _____

3. One day the children were disappointed because Pop didn't have something. What was that? _____

4. Why couldn't Pop get the truck fixed anymore?
   _____

5. Where had Pop taken the truck? _____

6. Who was in charge of the dump? _____

7. How did he use Pop's truck? _____

8. *Pop's Truck* is ▆▆▆ .
   - fiction
   - nonfiction

9. *Pop's Truck* is a ▆▆▆ .
   - play
   - story
   - poem

Lesson 40   11

## C SKILL ITEMS

**Match the objects with their new uses.**

A planter made out of •                               • an old bathtub

A dog house made out of •                         • an old refrigerator

A bookcase made out of •                          • an old boat

An office made out of •                               • an old truck

A cooler for water bottles made out of •     • an old table

## D REVIEW ITEMS

1. What do we call literature that is make-believe? _____

2. What do we call literature that is true? _____

3. Name the 3 main ways that literature is presented.
   _____

## E WRITING ITEMS

**Complete the sentence.**

No matter how old and worn out my _____

gets, I would never want to get rid of it.

**END OF LESSON 40**

# 41

Name _____

## A  INFORMATION ITEMS

1. Circle the names of 4 insects:
   - mouse
   - bee
   - toad
   - spider
   - ant
   - fish
   - snake
   - fly
   - turtle
   - beetle

2. How many parts does the body of an insect have? _____

3. How many parts does the body of an ant have? _____

4. All insects have _____ legs.

5. How many legs does a spider have? _____

6. How many parts does a spider's body have? _____

7. Is a spider an insect? _____

## B  STORY ITEMS

1. Mark New York City with the letters **NY**.

2. Mark San Francisco with the letters **SF**.

3. Draw an arrow from New York City to San Francisco.

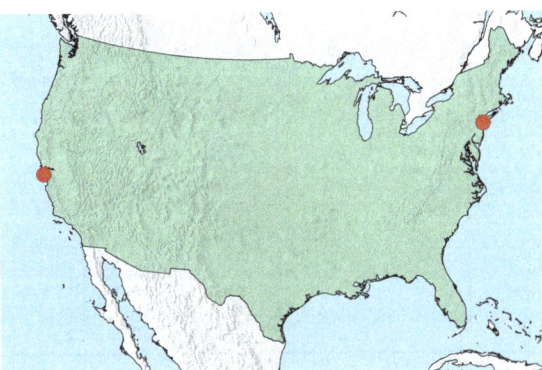

Lesson 41    13

4. How far would you travel to go from New York City to San Francisco? _____ miles

5. What did a passenger almost drop on Herman?
   • a purse    • a shoe    • a coat

6. When Herman flew away, he bumped into a living. What part of a living did he bump into?
   • a hand    • a face    • a coat

7. Herman got away by using a _____ -shaped move.

8. Who was telling the passengers what to do in case of danger?
   • the captain    • a flight attendant    • a grandmother

9. The flight attendants made sure that passengers were wearing ▮▮▮▮ .
   • seats    • coats    • seat belts

10. How many passengers were on the jumbo jet? _____

## C REVIEW ITEMS

The arrow in each picture shows which way the wind is blowing. Start at the dot and draw the smoke in each picture.

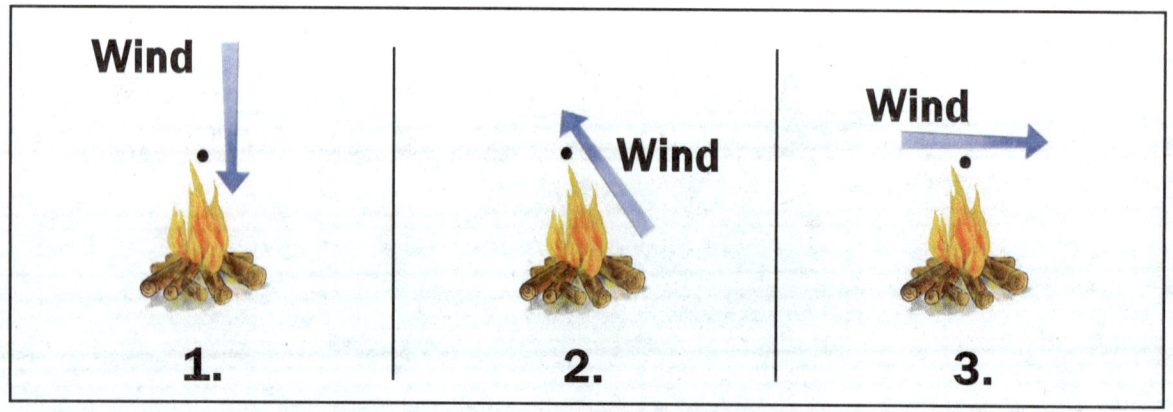

GO TO PART E IN YOUR TEXTBOOK

14   Lesson 41

# 42

## A  INFORMATION ITEMS

1. When we talk about how hot or cold something is, we tell about the _____ of the thing.

2. When an object gets hotter, the temperature goes _____ .

3. When the air gets cold, which way does the temperature go? _____

4. An oven gets hotter. So what do you know about the temperature of the oven?
   - It goes up.
   - It goes down.

---

The arrows show that the temperature is going up on thermometer A and going down on thermometer B.

5. In which picture is the water getting colder?
   - A
   - B

6. In which picture is the water getting hotter?
   - A
   - B

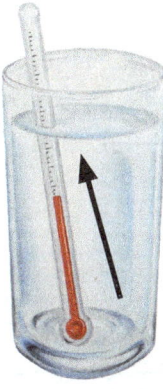
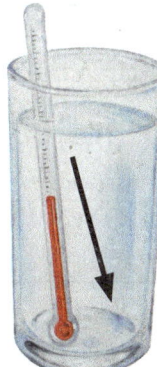

A          B

Lesson 42   15

## B  STORY ITEMS

1. The plane went up and up after it left New York City. How high did it go?
   - 5 miles
   - 6 miles
   - 100 miles

2. How fast does a jumbo jet fly?
   - 5 miles per hour
   - 6 miles per hour
   - 500 miles per hour

3. When a plane goes 5 hundred miles per hour, do the passengers feel that they're moving **fast** or **not at all**?
   - fast
   - not at all

4. How many flies were on the plane? _____

5. Which arrow shows the way the air will leave Goad's mouth? _____

6. Which arrow shows the way Goad will move? _____

7. Which arrow shows the way the air shoots from the jet engine? _____

8. Which arrow shows the way the jet moves? _____

**GO TO PART D IN YOUR TEXTBOOK**

16   Lesson 42

Name _____

## 43

### A  STORY ITEMS

1. Circle the city on the east coast that Herman flew from.
   - Chicago
   - New York City
   - San Francisco

2. Circle the city on the west coast that Herman flew to.
   - Chicago
   - New York City
   - San Francisco

3. How far is the trip from New York to San Francisco?
   _____

4. The kitchen on an airplane is called ▇▇▇ .
   - a kitchen
   - a galley
   - a garage

5. Herman went from New York City to San Francisco. Circle 3 cities he flew over.
   - Chicago
   - Denver
   - New England
   - Lake Michigan
   - Alaska
   - Salt Lake City

6. Circle the pictures that show what Herman had for his meal service.

A   B   C   D   E   F

Lesson 43

7. Herman took a nap on something. What was that thing?

   • a wooden panel   • a plastic panel   • a metal panel

8. Why did Herman like that place?

   • It was quiet.   • It was warm.   • It was smooth.

9. Write **east** next to the city on the east coast.

10. Write **west** next to the city on the west coast.

11. Draw an arrow that shows the trip the jet plane took.

12. Make a **D** where Denver is.

13. Make a **C** where Chicago is.

14. How many flies were on the plane when it left New York City? ____

15. How many flies got off the plane in San Francisco? ____

**GO TO PART D IN YOUR TEXTBOOK**

18   Lesson 43

Name _____

**44**

## A INFORMATION ITEMS

1. Write **north**, **south**, **east**, and **west** in the shaded boxes.

2. Write the letter of the animal that is facing into the wind. _____

3. Which direction is that animal facing? _____

4. So what's the name of the wind? _____ wind

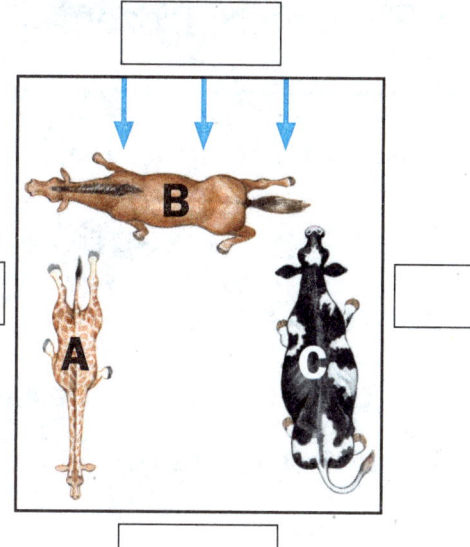

## B STORY ITEMS

1. How many flies were on the plane when it left New York City? _____

2. How many flies got off the plane in San Francisco? _____

3. How many flies died on the plane? _____

4. What killed them?
   • Herman     • fly spray     • cold air

5. When fly spray filled the air, Herman was near ▨.
   • an open door     • a red seat     • a window

6. The air that blew on Herman was ▨.
   • filled with fly spray     • fresh air     • hot air

Lesson 44  19

7. Some workers stacked dinners in the galley. Why didn't those dinners smell very good to Herman?
   - They were rotten.
   - They were small.
   - They were frozen.

Look at the map below. The **Y** shows where the wind starts.

8. Write **north, south, east,** and **west** in the boxes.
9. Make a **Z** where San Francisco is.
10. If you were in San Francisco, which direction would you face if you wanted the wind to blow in your face? _____

GO TO PART D IN YOUR TEXTBOOK

20   Lesson 44

Name _____

45

## A  INFORMATION ITEMS

The arrows in each picture show which way the wind is blowing.

1. **Draw a circle** around the plane in each picture that will go the fastest.

2. **Draw an arrow** on the cloud in each picture to show which direction it is moving.

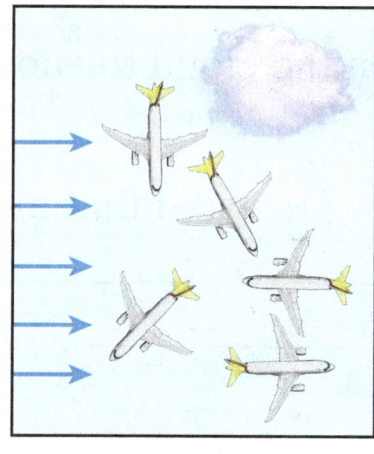
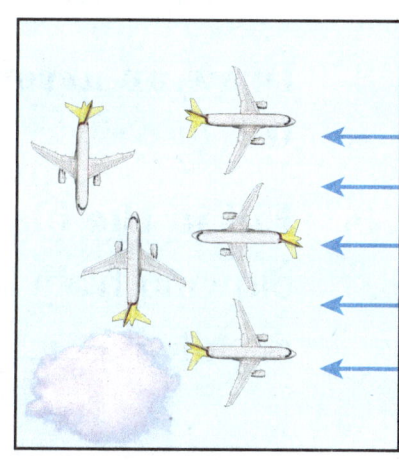

**PICTURE 1**    **PICTURE 2**    **PICTURE 3**

## B  STORY ITEMS

1. How long did the trip to San Francisco take? _____

2. How long did the trip back to New York City take? _____

3. The trip back to New York City took less time because the plane went in ▨ .

   • the same direction as the wind
   • the opposite direction as the wind

Lesson 45    21

4. What month was it when Herman landed in San Francisco?
   • May    • June    • July

5. What was the temperature when Herman landed in San Francisco? _____ degrees

6. Was it hotter or colder in San Francisco when the plane left?

_____

7. Write **north, south, east,** and **west** in the boxes.

8. **Draw an arrow** on the cloud to show which way the cloud will move.

9. **Fill in the blanks.** The wind that moves the cloud is blowing from the _____ . So that wind is called a _____ .

22    Lesson 45

10. What made the trip to New York City a rough trip?
    - the captain
    - the copilot
    - the clouds

11. Why did the captain tell the passengers to keep their seat belts fastened?
    - because of meal service
    - because of rough air
    - because of low temperature

12. Did the passengers enjoy the trip?   • yes   • no

13. Circle 2 words that tell how most passengers felt.
    - happy
    - sick
    - sleepy
    - frightened
    - hungry

**GO TO PART D IN YOUR TEXTBOOK**

# 46

**A  INFORMATION ITEMS**

1. Write **north, south, east,** and **west** in the right boxes.
2. Make an **H** where New York City is.
3. Make an **F** where San Francisco is.
4. Make a **J** where Japan is.
5. Make a **P** where the Pacific Ocean is.

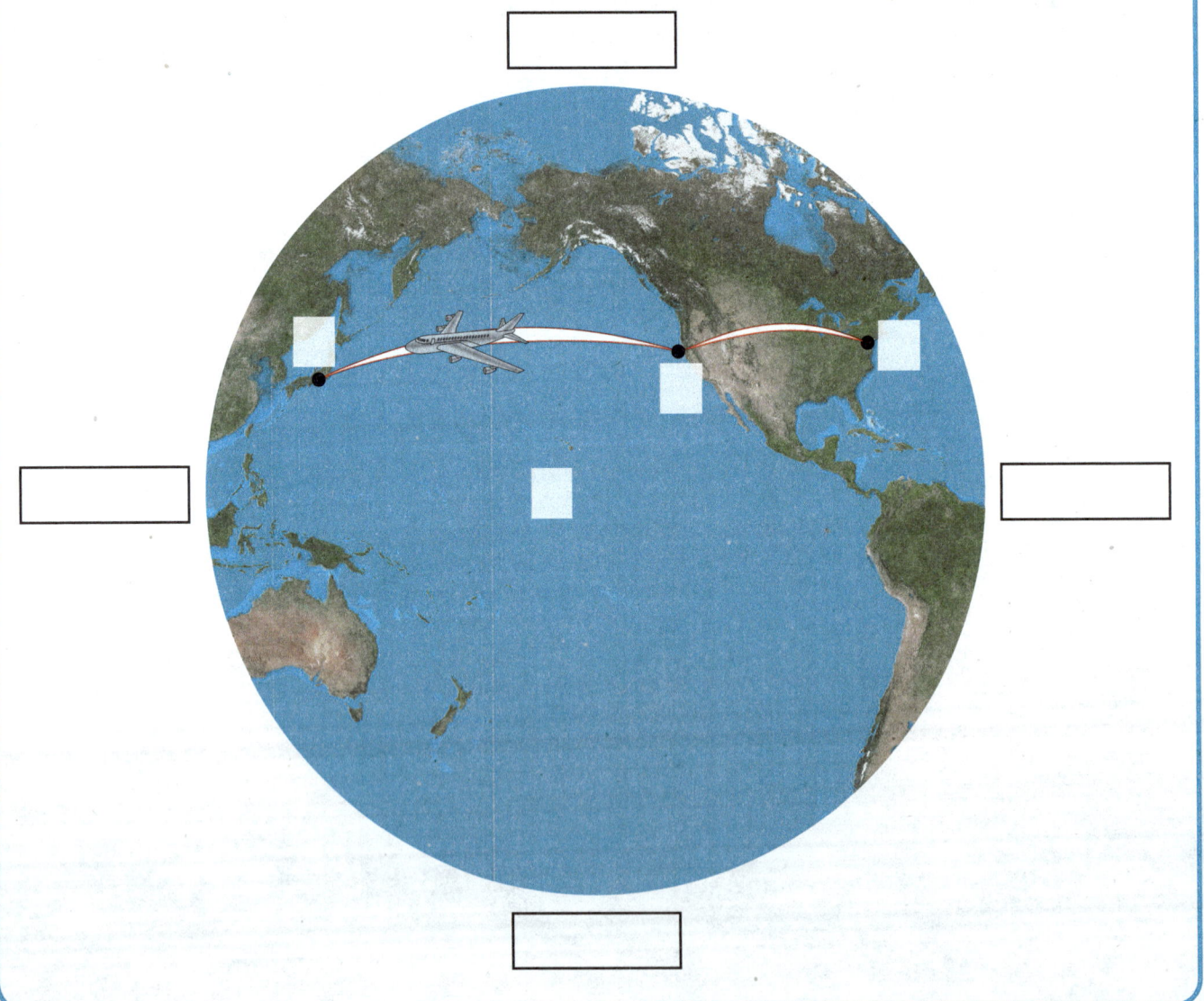

Lesson 46

## B STORY ITEMS

1. Did the fly spray kill Herman? _____

2. Where was Herman when fly spray filled the air?
   - on a paper panel
   - inside an oven
   - on a red seat

3. After the plane left New York City, where did it stop first?
   - Japan
   - Chicago
   - San Francisco

4. Then the plane left for ▇▇▇ .
   - Japan
   - Chicago
   - San Francisco

5. In what direction did the plane fly? _____

6. How far is it from New York City to San Francisco?
   _____ miles

7. How far is it from San Francisco to Japan?
   _____ miles

8. What ocean do you cross to get from San Francisco to Japan?
   - Alaska
   - Pacific
   - Peaceful

9. What did Herman get stuck in? _____

10. **Cross out** Herman's enemy.

A

B

C

**GO TO PART D IN YOUR TEXTBOOK**

# 47  Name _____

## A  INFORMATION ITEMS

1. Which eye works like one drop, a human's eye or a fly's eye?
   - human eye
   - fly eye

2. Which eye works like many drops?
   - human eye
   - fly eye

3. Which eye can see more things at the same time?
   - human eye
   - fly eye

## B  STORY ITEMS

1. When a spider wraps an insect in a web, the insect looks like a ▢ .
   - fly
   - mummy
   - spider

2. **Circle** the spider.

3. **Cross out** Herman.

4. **Make a box** around the dead insect.

## C REVIEW ITEMS

1. Write **north, south, east,** and **west** in the right boxes.
2. Is the United States shown on this map? _____
3. Which letter shows where New York City is? _____
4. Which letter shows where San Francisco is? _____
5. Which letter shows where Japan is? _____
6. Which letter shows where the Pacific Ocean is? _____

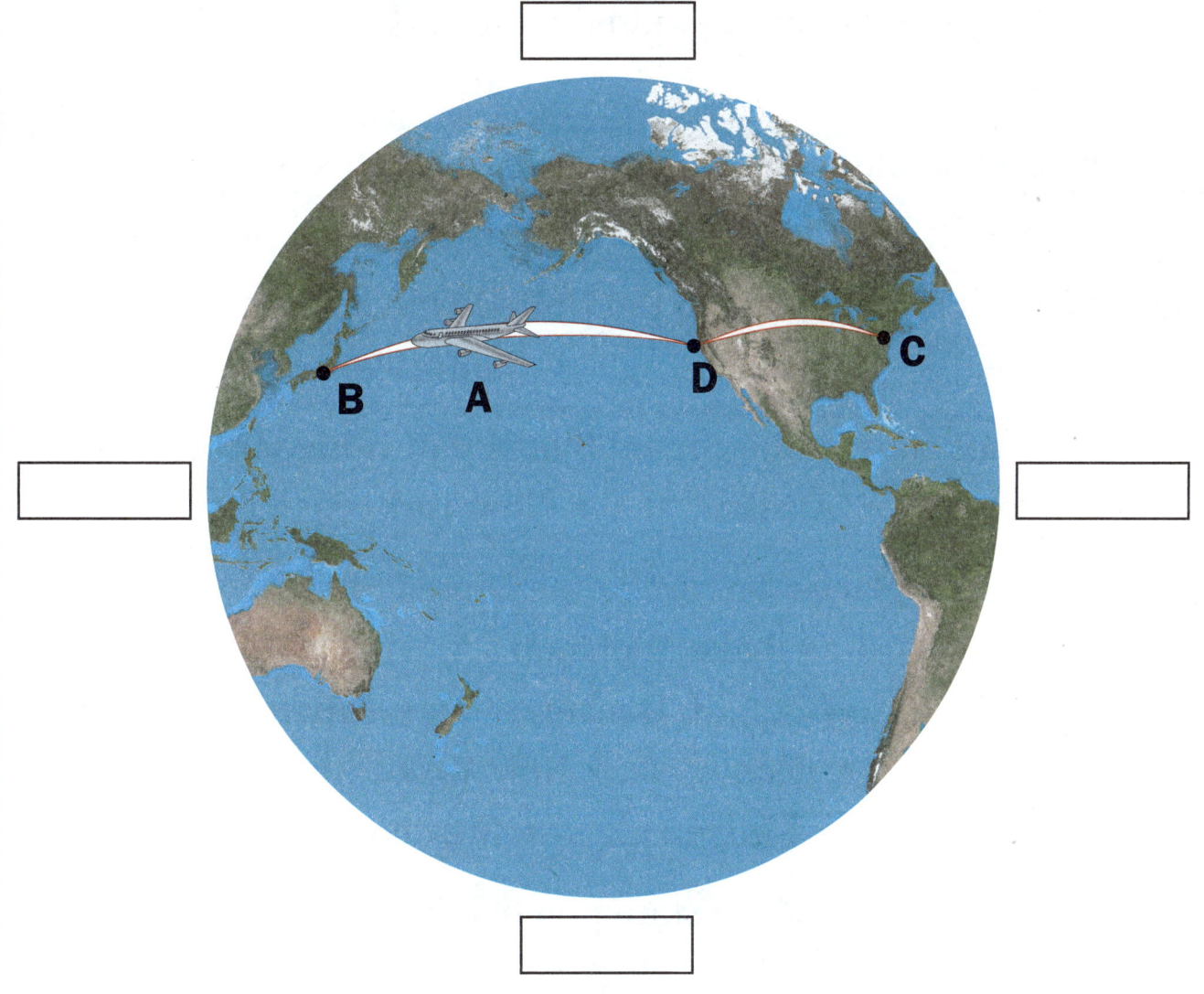

**GO TO PART D IN YOUR TEXTBOOK**

Lesson 47

# 48

**A** INFORMATION ITEMS

1. The United States is a ▭ .
   - state
   - country
   - city

2. Japan is a ▭ .
   - state
   - country
   - city

3. The United States is made up of fifty ▭ .
   - countries
   - cities
   - states

4. The biggest state in the United States is ▭ .
   - Texas
   - Alaska
   - California

5. The second biggest state in the United States is ▭ .
   - Texas
   - Alaska
   - California

6. The third biggest state in the United States is ▭ .
   - Texas
   - Alaska
   - California

7. Circle the state in the United States that is bigger than Japan.
   - Ohio
   - Alaska
   - New York

8. Circle the 9 places that are in the United States.
   - Chicago
   - Lake Michigan
   - California
   - San Francisco
   - Denver
   - Japan
   - Texas
   - Ohio
   - New York City
   - Alaska
   - Canada
   - Mexico

9. What's the name of the state you live in? _____

## B  STORY ITEMS

1. What country is shown in the picture? _____

2. What did Herman do after he escaped from the spider?
   • took a nap    • ate candy    • flew into a closet

3. The plane landed in the country of _____.

4. Why were the passengers excited about landing there?
   • They were hungry.
   • They had been on the plane for many hours.
   • They were tired.

5. A passenger told the others that the tiny lines they saw showed where ▭ .
   • the ocean was
   • the mountains were
   • the airport was

**GO TO PART E IN YOUR TEXTBOOK**

## A  STORY ITEMS

1. Let's say that you are outside when the temperature is 50 degrees. What is the temperature inside your body?
   - 50 degrees
   - 90 degrees
   - 98 degrees

2. Let's say you are outside when it is 90 degrees. What is the temperature inside your body?
   - 50 degrees
   - 90 degrees
   - 98 degrees

3. Let's say a fly is outside when the temperature is 50 degrees. What is the temperature inside the fly's body?
   - 50 degrees
   - 90 degrees
   - 98 degrees

4. Let's say a fly is outside when the temperature is 90 degrees. What is the temperature inside the fly's body?
   - 50 degrees
   - 90 degrees
   - 98 degrees

5. Herman wanted to get out of the jet because ▓ .
   - he was old
   - he was cold
   - he was hungry

6. Would it be easier to catch a fly on a hot day or on a cold day?
   - hot day
   - cold day

7. Tell why.
   - because the fly is moving slowly
   - because the fly is hungry
   - because the fly is moving quickly

Circle **warm-blooded** or **cold-blooded** for each animal.

8. Herman warm-blooded cold-blooded
9. fly warm-blooded cold-blooded
10. ant warm-blooded cold-blooded
11. dog warm-blooded cold-blooded
12. cat warm-blooded cold-blooded
13. flea warm-blooded cold-blooded
14. spider warm-blooded cold-blooded
15. horse warm-blooded cold-blooded

## B  REVIEW ITEMS

1. Write **north**, **south**, **east**, and **west** in the right boxes.
2. Make an **F** where San Francisco is.
3. Make a **C** where Chicago is.
4. Make an **X** where New York City is.

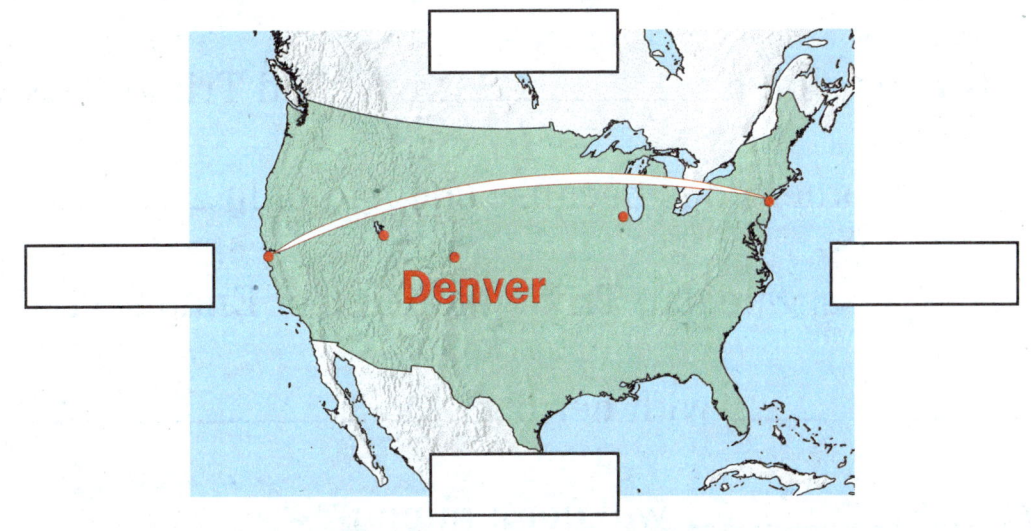

**GO TO PART C IN YOUR TEXTBOOK**

# 50  Name _____

## A  BEGINNING, MIDDLE, END

Put a 1 after the thing that happened at the beginning.
Put a 2 after the thing that happened in the middle of the story.
Put a 3 after the thing that happened at the end.

  a. Emma met her puppy. _____
  b. Emma couldn't find Trixie and Gus at the dump. _____
  c. Emma met Trixie for the first time. _____

## B  SETTING, CHARACTERS, PLOT

**Answer these questions about the story *Trixie*.**

1. What is the setting for this story? _____

2. Name the 2 main characters in this story. _____

3. **Complete the plot for this story. Write the missing words.**

   This story is about a girl named _____ who became friends with a _____ named Trixie. Trixie was different from other dogs because she had only _____s. One day Trixie didn't meet Emma. Trixie was in the _____ with her 6 _____. In two months, _____ will get a puppy.

## C. AUTHOR'S PURPOSE

Match the author's purpose to each title. Circle **persuade, entertain,** or **explain.**

1. How to Start a Garden — persuade   entertain   explain
2. Why You Should Shave Your Head — persuade   entertain   explain
3. Six Monkeys on a Baseball Team — persuade   entertain   explain
4. Baking a Cake Made Easy — persuade   entertain   explain
5. A Thousand Tears and Smiles — persuade   entertain   explain
6. Fixing Your Car — persuade   entertain   explain
7. What You Need to Know About the Ocean — persuade   entertain   explain
8. Always Vote for the Woman — persuade   entertain   explain
9. A Vacation for 50 Dollars per Day — persuade   entertain   explain
10. Love Story — persuade   entertain   explain

## D STORY ITEMS

1. What was unusual about Trixie? _____

2. How did Trixie get hurt? _____

3. Where does Emma see Trixie? _____

4. Who owns Trixie? _____

5. Name 2 things that Emma liked to do with Trixie.
   _____

6. What surprise did Trixie have for Gus and Emma?
   _____

7. What was Emma going to get from Trixie?
   _____

**END OF LESSON 50**

Name _____

# 51

## A  INFORMATION ITEMS

1. Jean is 2 miles high. Fran is 5 miles high. Who is colder?

   _____

2. Tell why.
   - because she is colder
   - because she is higher
   - because she is lower

## B  STORY ITEMS

1. How far is the trip from Japan to Italy?
   - 6 hundred miles
   - 6 thousand miles
   - 60 thousand miles

2. How long should that trip take?
   - 6 hours
   - 12 hours
   - 13 hours

3. Circle 2 countries the plane flew over on the trip.
   - Turkey
   - United States
   - Canada
   - England
   - China

4. Circle the state in the United States that is bigger than Italy.
   - Ohio
   - Alaska
   - New York

5. Italy is shaped something like a ▬ .
   - horn
   - shoe
   - boot

6. When could Herman move fastest?
   - when it is 60 degrees
   - when it is 80 degrees
   - when it is 50 degrees
   - when it is 45 degrees

7. Write **north, south, east,** and **west** in the right boxes.

8. Make a **J** where Japan is.

9. Make a **C** where China is.

10. Make a **T** where Turkey is.

11. Make an **I** where Italy is.

12. Is the United States shown on this map? _____

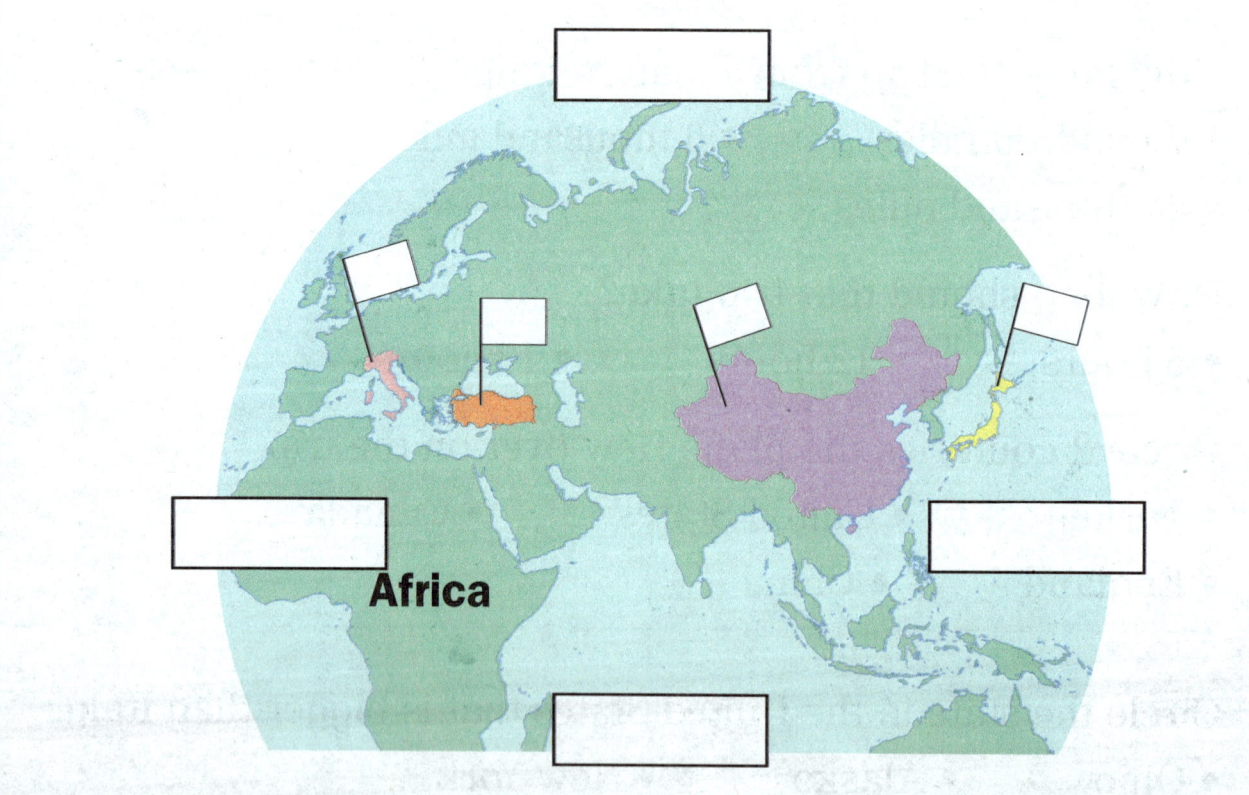

Name _____

## A STORY ITEMS

1. **Circle 2** of the things below that would smell very good to Herman.

2. **Underline** one thing that would smell bad to Herman.

   • meat     • soap     • candy     • garbage     • gum

3. A plane that flies from Italy to New York City goes in which direction? _____

4. What airport did Herman fly to in this story?
   • San Francisco     • Kennedy     • Italy

5. In what city is that airport?
   • Chicago     • San Francisco     • New York City

6. Where are the fuel tanks on a big jet?
   • in the rear     • in the wings     • in the galley

7. It was hard for Herman to move around in the fall because ▓▓▓ .
   • it was raining     • the temperature went up
   • the temperature went down

8. What killed Herman?
   • freezing     • boiling     • sleeping

Lesson 52    37

9. Which letter shows where Italy is? _____

10. Which letter shows where New York City is? _____

11. Which letter shows where Turkey is? _____

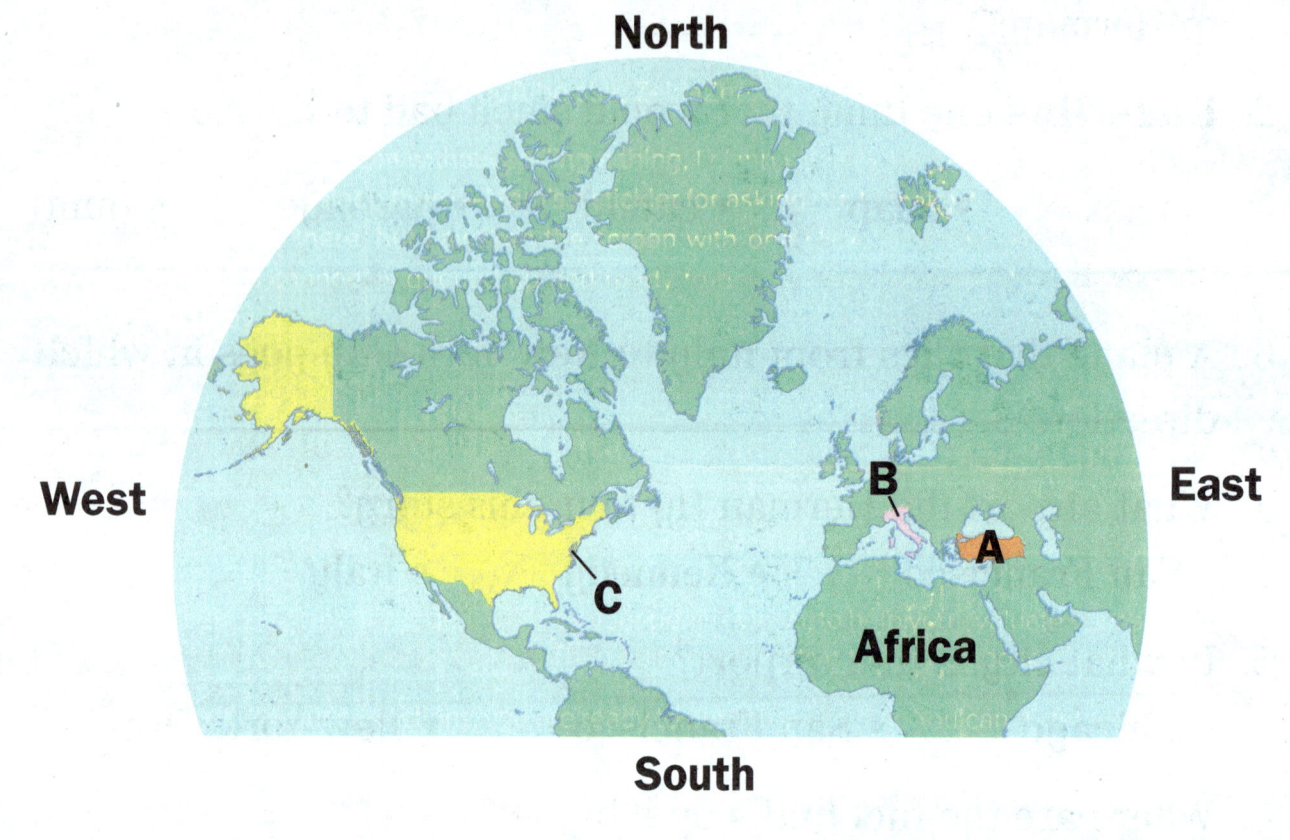

## B  REVIEW ITEMS

1. Ann is 10 miles high. Bob is 6 miles high. Who is colder?
   _____

2. Tell why. _____

GO TO PART C IN YOUR TEXTBOOK

# 53

**Name** _____

## A  INFORMATION ITEMS—PASSAGE 1

The picture shows 4 objects caught in a whirlpool.

1. Write **1** on the object that will go down the hole in the whirlpool first.

2. Write **2** on the object that will go down next.

3. Number the rest of the objects.

4. Circle the rule about how close an object is to a drain and how fast it moves.

   a. The closer it is to the drain, the faster it goes.

   b. The farther it is from the drain, the faster it goes.

   c. The closer it is to the drain, the slower it goes.

Lesson 53

## B INFORMATION ITEMS—PASSAGE 2

1. Put a **B** on 2 bulkheads.
2. Put an **X** on 2 decks.
3. Put a **W** at the bow.
4. Put an **S** at the stern.

## C INFORMATION ITEMS—PASSAGE 3

The picture below shows jars of water on a very cold day.

32 degrees   32 degrees   32 degrees   32 degrees   32 degrees   32 degrees

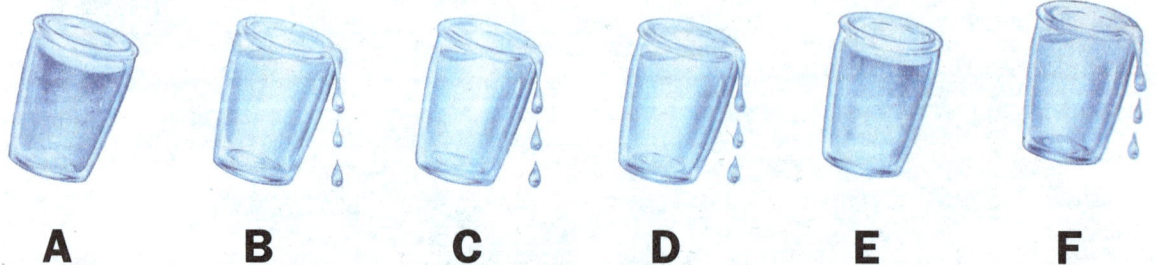

A    B    C    D    E    F

1. What is the temperature of the water in each jar?

_____

2. Write **OW** on each jar that is filled with ocean water.

3. Jar F is filled with ocean water. How do you know?

_____

**GO TO PART F IN YOUR TEXTBOOK**

Name _____

## A POEM ITEM

She drew a picture on the wall,
    And one more on the door.
She couldn't reach up very high,

_____

## B STORY ITEMS

1. Linda and Kathy were on a ship that was going from the United States to ▨ .

    • Canada    • England    • Japan

2. The girls were on their way to visit their _____ .

3. Did Linda and Kathy go in one of the lifeboats when the ship sank? _____

4. What did the girls plan to use for a lifeboat?

    • a raft    • a crate    • a boat

5. Which girl could swim well?    • Linda    • Kathy

6. Which girl was older? _____

7. How much older? _____

8. When the ship sank, it was in the middle of the _____ Ocean.

9. A stranger lifted ▨ into a lifeboat.

    • Linda    • Kathy

Lesson 54   41

10. Why didn't she stay in the lifeboat?
   - She went to find her sister.
   - She was scared.
   - She couldn't swim.

## C  REVIEW ITEMS

1. Write **north, south, east,** and **west** in the right boxes.

2. Which letter shows where Japan is? _____

3. Which letter shows where Italy is? _____

4. Which letter shows where Turkey is? _____

5. Which letter shows where China is? _____

6. Is the United States shown on this map? _____

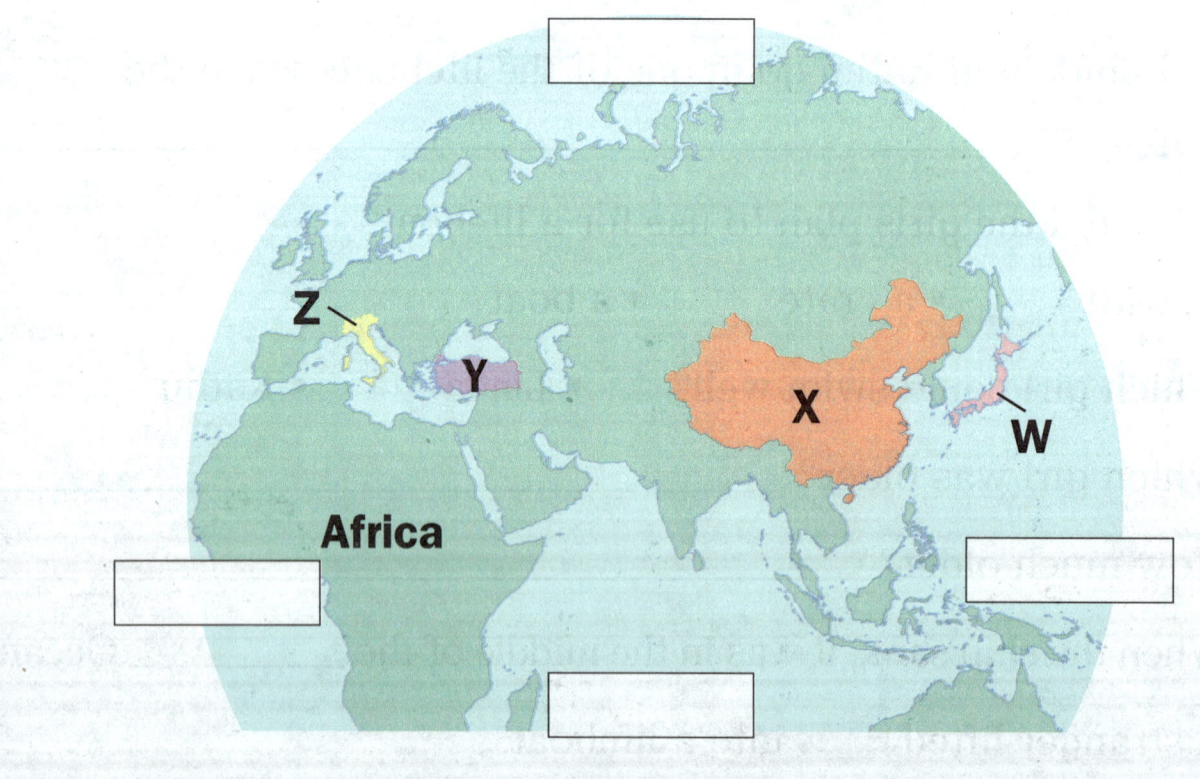

**GO TO PART C IN YOUR TEXTBOOK**

42   Lesson 54

Name _____

## A POEM ITEM

He walked down the street;

    Thump thump thump.

He listened to his feet;

_____ .

## B STORY ITEMS

1. Why did Linda have a hard time swimming to the crate?
   - She could not swim well.
   - Currents held her back.
   - She was weak.

2. What did Linda and Kathy use for a lifeboat? _____

3. What did the girls use for paddles?
   - oars
   - hands
   - boards

4. What made Linda's feet sore?
   - the crate
   - the salt water
   - the sun

5. If you drank lots of ocean water, you would get ▬▬ .
   - hungry
   - tired
   - thirstier

Lesson 55

Here's a picture of Kathy and Linda on their crate.

6. Which arrow shows the way Linda's hand will move? _____
7. Which arrow shows the way the crate will move? _____

8. Something made sounds that told Linda they were near the shore. What made those sounds?

    • waves on the beach      • birds in the trees

    • fish in the waves

9. As the girls walked along the beach, they could hardly see where they were going. Tell why. _____

## C  REVIEW ITEMS

1. Write **north, south, east,** and **west** in the right boxes.

2. Which letter shows where China is? _____

3. Which letter shows where Japan is? _____

4. Is the United States shown on this map? _____

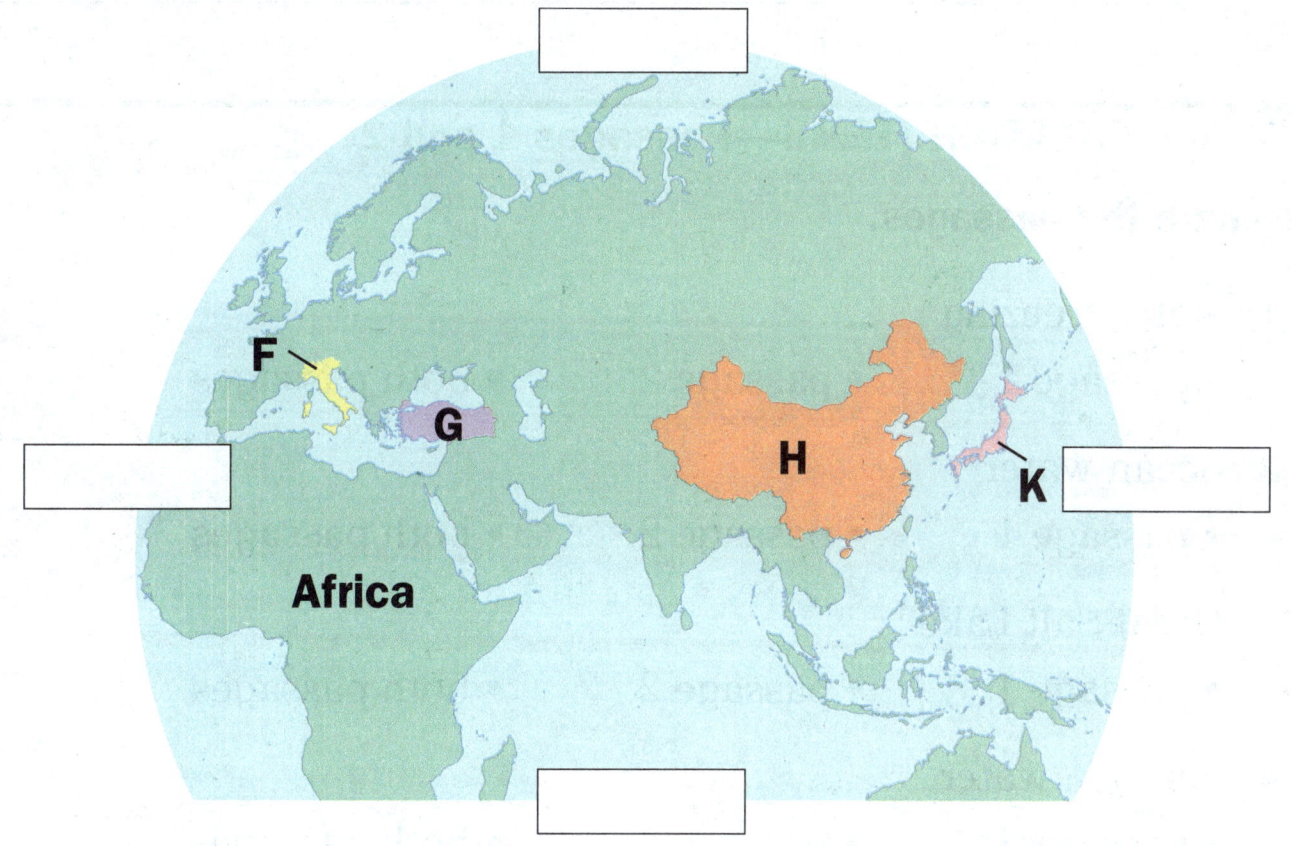

**GO TO PART E IN YOUR TEXTBOOK**

Lesson 55   45

## A POEM ITEM

I say a simple poem

   In every place I roam.

I whisper it in school;

   And _____.

## B INFORMATION ITEMS—Passages 1 and 2

**Compare the passages.**

1. water freezing
   - passage 1
   - passage 2
   - both passages

2. ocean water
   - passage 1
   - passage 2
   - both passages

3. Great Salt Lake
   - passage 1
   - passage 2
   - both passages

4. corks in water
   - passage 1
   - passage 2
   - both passages

5. fresh water
   - passage 1
   - passage 2
   - both passages

## C  STORY ITEMS

The map shows the island that Linda and Kathy were on.

1. Write **north, south, east,** and **west** in the right boxes.

2. **Draw a line** from the crate to show where Linda and Kathy walked.

3. **Make an X** to show where Linda was when she saw footprints.

4. **Make a Y** to show where they landed on the island.

5. **Make an S** to show where the stream is.

6. **Circle** the grove where they found bananas.

**GO TO PART E IN YOUR TEXTBOOK**

Lesson 56

# 57

## A POEM ITEM

My sister has a truck that's old;
   She drives it once a week.
The engine doesn't run too well;
_____

## B STORY ITEMS

The picture shows a coconut.

1. Make an **X** on the part that the girls ate.
2. Make a **Y** on the part that the girls drank.

3. What was wrong with the first coconuts that the girls found?
   - They were too high in the trees.
   - They were not ripe.
   - They were rotten.

4. When Kathy shook the coconut, it sounded like a bottle that had water in it. What made the sound like water? _____

5. What did Linda and Kathy use to open the coconut? _____

6. Why did the girls want to make the monkeys mad?
   - so they would throw coconuts
   - so they would go away
   - so they would make noise

## C REVIEW ITEMS

The map shows the island that Linda and Kathy were on.

1. Write **north, south, east,** and **west** in the right boxes.
2. **Draw a line** from the crate to show where Linda and Kathy walked.
3. **Make an A** to show where Linda was when she saw footprints.
4. **Make a B** to show where they landed on the island.
5. **Make a C** to show where the stream is.
6. **Circle** the grove where they found bananas.

**GO TO PART D IN YOUR TEXTBOOK**

Lesson 57

# 58  Name _____

## A INFORMATION ITEMS

1. All machines make it easier for someone to _____ .

2. You would have the most power if you pushed against handle C.

   Which handle would give you the least amount of power? ___

3. When the author told about machines, was the purpose to **persuade, explain,** or **entertain**? _____

## B  STORY ITEMS

1. What were the only things Linda and Kathy ate for two days?
   - carrots
   - coconuts
   - corn
   - fronds
   - cabbage
   - bananas

2. Why did Linda and Kathy want to catch some fish?
   - They were tired.
   - They wanted to eat something new.
   - They could not open the coconuts.

3. What did they use for fish hooks? _____

4. What did they use for a fishing line? _____

5. Were there many fish in the water? _____

6. Did Linda and Kathy catch many fish with their hooks and lines? _____

7. The girls made hooks and lines to catch fish. Then they made something else to catch fish. What else did they make? _____

8. What did they make it out of? _____

9. What happened when the girls tried to pull the net out of the water?
   - The fish jumped out of the water.
   - The fish pulled the girls into the water.
   - The crate fell in the water.

**GO TO PART D IN YOUR TEXTBOOK**

Lesson 58

## A  STORY ITEMS

1. At the beginning of today's story, Linda and Kathy had a big problem. What was that problem?
   - They were hungry.
   - They needed a crate to paddle away from the island.
   - The fish net was too heavy to pull out of the water.

2. Linda's idea to solve the problem was to ▬▬ .
   - build a machine
   - make more fish hooks
   - eat coconuts

3. What did the girls find floating in the water?
   - a ship
   - a first-aid kit
   - boards

4. The white box probably came from ▬▬ .
   - their ship
   - their crate
   - Italy

5. What was the most important thing inside the box?
   - candy
   - food
   - matches

6. Why didn't the girls test them right away?
   - They would need them later.
   - They didn't know how.
   - They were tired.

7. The girls made a ▬▬ .
   - building
   - machine
   - motor

8. What did the girls use for a handle?
   - a board
   - a log
   - a vine

52  Lesson 59

9. The girls hammered the handle to the end of ▇.
   - a shoe
   - a log
   - a crate

10. The girls got nails from ▇.
    - a shoe
    - a log
    - a crate

11. They tie one end of the vine to the log and the other end of the vine to the ▇.
    - beach
    - crate
    - net

12. When the fish were in the net, the girls ▇.
    - turned the handle
    - ran into the water
    - climbed a tree

13. The arrow by the handle shows which way it turns. Start at the dot on the log. Make an arrow on the log to show which way it turns.

14. Make an arrow by the vine to show which way it moves.

**GO TO PART C IN YOUR TEXTBOOK**

Lesson 59   53

## 60  Name _____

### A  SETTING, CHARACTERS, PLOT

Answer these questions about the story *The Three Wishes.*

1. What are the two settings for this story?
   _____

2. Who are the two main characters in this story?
   _____

3. Complete the plot for this story. Write the missing words.

   A _____ gave a man and his wife _____ wishes. Their first _____ was a pan of sausages. Their next wish was sausages on the man's _____. Finally they wished the sausages would get _____ his nose. Then they sat down to a fine dinner of _____.

### B  STORY ITEMS

1. Who gave the man and his wife three wishes? _____

2. Why did he give them the wishes?
   _____

54  Lesson 60

3. Name 3 things the man and his wife talked about wishing for.

   1. _____
   2. _____
   3. _____

4. Who made the first wish? _____

5. What did he wish for? _____

6. Who made the second wish? _____

7. What was the second wish?

   _____

8. What problem did the man and his wife have near the end of the story?
   - There were sausages hanging from the man's nose.
   - They were hungry.
   - They had no more wood to cut.

9. How did they solve their problem?
   - They cut off the sausages.
   - They used their third wish.
   - They ate.

10. Who made the third wish? _____

11. What was the third wish?

    _____

Lesson 60

12. Were the man and his wife **happy** or **sad** at the end of the story?
    _____

13. Why did they feel that way?
    _____
    _____

## C  SKILL ITEMS

1. *The Three Wishes* is ▆▆ and ▆▆ .
   - nonfiction
   - fiction
   - a poem
   - a folktale
   - a riddle story

2. *The Little Red House With a Star Inside* is ▆▆ , ▆▆ , and ▆▆ .
   - nonfiction
   - fiction
   - a poem
   - a folktale
   - a riddle story

3. *Facts About Machines* is ▆▆ .
   - nonfiction
   - fiction
   - a poem
   - a folktale
   - a riddle story

**GO TO PART D IN YOUR TEXTBOOK**

Name _____

**61**

## A  INFORMATION ITEMS

1. What is it called when the sun goes down?
   - sunrise
   - sunset

2. What is it called when the sun comes up?
   - sunrise
   - sunset

## B  STORY ITEMS

1. What did Kathy have to do to the outside of the fish?
   - remove fins
   - remove scales
   - remove shells

2. What did she use for a tool?
   - a fin
   - a scale
   - a shell

3. What was Linda's job when the girls cleaned the fish?
   - removing the scales
   - removing the insides
   - removing the fins

4. What did she use for a tool?
   - a belt buckle
   - a nail
   - a rock

5. Linda made her tool sharp by ▭ .
   - rubbing it against a rock
   - putting it in the fire
   - making it red hot

6. Name 2 things the girls ate for dinner.

   1 _____

   2 _____

Lesson 61

7. Linda and Kathy drank fresh water with their dinner.

   Where did they get the fresh water? _____

8. Circle 4 things that the girls used to make their simple machine.
   - vines
   - nails
   - coconuts
   - boards
   - rope
   - a tree trunk
   - turtle shell
   - matches

## C  REVIEW ITEMS

1. The arrow by the handle shows which way the handle turns. Make an arrow on the log to show which way the log moves. Start at the dot.

2. Make an arrow by the vine to show which way the vine moves.

**GO TO PART D IN YOUR TEXTBOOK**

58     Lesson 61

Name _____

## A  INFORMATION ITEMS—Passages 1 and 2

**Compare the passages.**

1. palm trees
   - passage 1
   - passage 2
   - both passages

2. 2 thousand kinds of palm trees
   - passage 1
   - passage 2
   - both passages

3. sea coconut
   - passage 1
   - passage 2
   - both passages

4. coconuts that weigh 40 pounds
   - passage 1
   - passage 2
   - both passages

5. fronds
   - passage 1
   - passage 2
   - both passages

6. banana plants
   - passage 1
   - passage 2
   - both passages

## B  INFORMATION ITEMS

1. The temperature inside your body is about _____ degrees.

2. Most fevers don't go over _____ degrees.

3. When people have very high fevers, they may see and hear things that are not _____ .

## C  STORY ITEMS

1. How long had Linda and Kathy been on the island when they saw the airplane?
   - 15 days
   - 3 weeks
   - 12 days

2. Did the people in the plane see Linda and Kathy? _____

3. What did the girls use to make a signal for planes?
   - paint
   - rocks
   - leaves

4. What word did they spell? _____

5. The word was more than _____ feet long.

6. What kind of signal did the girls have ready for ships?
   - rocks
   - fog
   - smoke

7. What would make the fire smoke?
   - sticks
   - green leaves
   - bananas

8. How did Linda know that Kathy had a fever?
   - Linda felt her forehead.
   - Linda took her temperature.
   - Linda felt her feet.

9. Linda thought that Kathy's temperature was over _____ degrees.

## D  REVIEW ITEMS

1. The United States is a _____.
   - city
   - state
   - country

2. Japan is a _____.

3. How many states are in the United States? _____

**GO TO PART E IN YOUR TEXTBOOK**

Lesson 62

Name _____

63

### A  INFORMATION ITEMS

1. Put a **T** next to each tugboat.
2. Put a **D** on each dock.
3. Put an **S** next to each ship.

### B  STORY ITEMS

1. How long had Linda and Kathy been on the island when they saw the airplane?
   - 15 days
   - 3 weeks
   - 12 days

2. Did the people in the plane see Linda and Kathy? _____

Lesson 63    61

3. What did the girls use to make a signal for planes?
   • paint      • rocks      • leaves

4. What word did they spell? _____

5. The word was over _____ feet long.

6. What kind of signal did the girls have ready for ships?
   • rocks      • fog      • smoke

7. What made the fire smoke so much?
   • sticks      • green leaves      • bananas

8. What was the name of the ship that rescued the girls?
   • S. S. Mason      • S. S. Milton      • S. S. Sisters

9. Kathy's forehead was hot because she had a _____ .

10. How long were the girls on the island?
    • one week      • 2 weeks      • almost 3 weeks

11. How long were the girls on the S.S. Milton?
    • one week      • 2 weeks      • almost 3 weeks

12. Where did the S.S. Milton take them? _____

13. Who took them to their new home? _____

14. Did Linda think it would be dull there? _____

Lesson 63

15. Linda showed Captain Allen 4 things that she and Kathy had used to survive on the island. Circle those 4 things.
    - machine
    - belt buckle
    - table
    - books
    - TV
    - wagon
    - house
    - socks
    - bathtub
    - fish net
    - vines

16. Captain Allen was ▓▓▓ .
    - worried
    - amazed
    - angry

## C REVIEW ITEMS

1. The temperature inside your body is about _____ degrees when your body is healthy.

2. Most fevers don't go over _____ degrees.

**GO TO PART D IN YOUR TEXTBOOK**

# 64  Name _____

## A  PASSAGE 2 ITEMS

Match the numbers to the places. Use the map.

1. •         • Where Greece is.
2. •         • Where Italy is.
3. •         • Where Troy used to be.

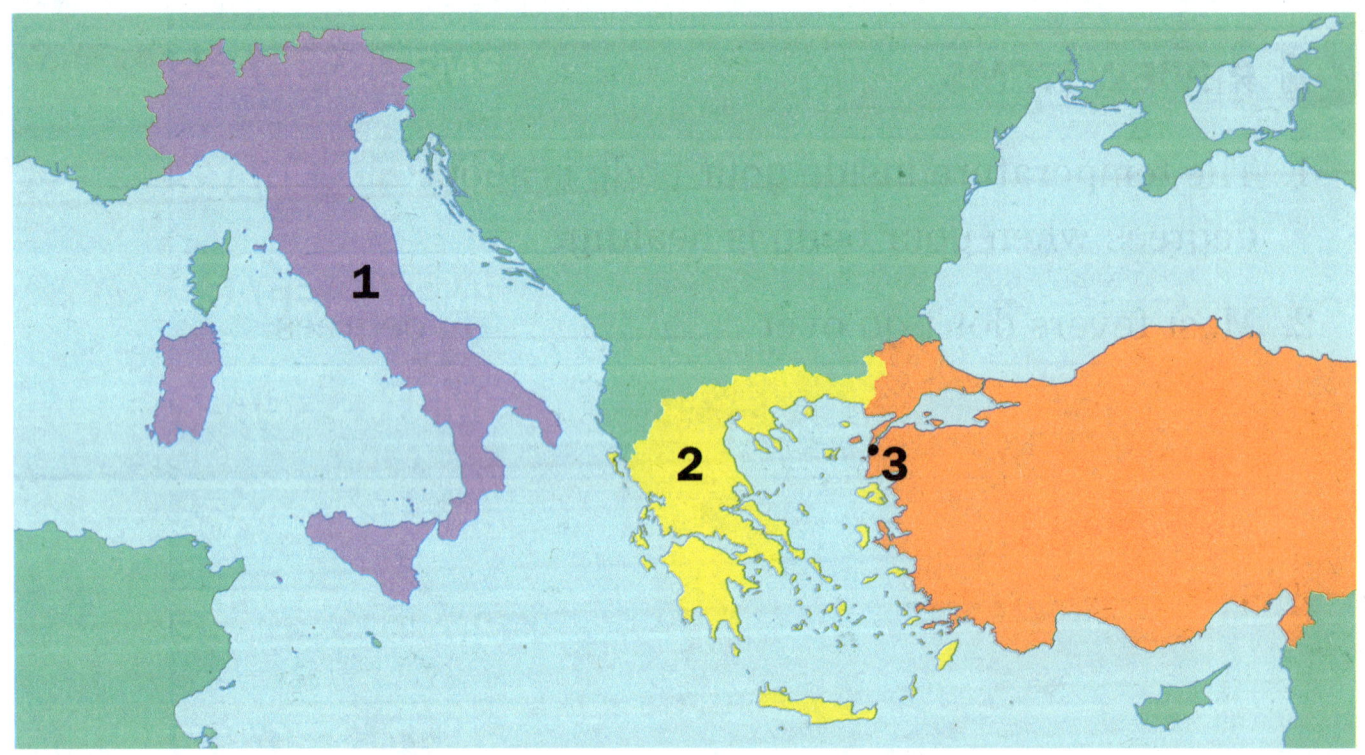

4. The place that was called Troy is now part of what country?
   • Italy      • Greece      • Turkey

## B  PASSAGE 3 ITEMS

1. What year is it now? _____
2. In what year were you born? _____
3. In what year was the first airplane made? _____

4. What was the year 1 hundred years ago?
   _____

5. What was the year 2 hundred years ago?
   _____

6. In what year did the United States become a country?
   _____

7. What was the year 3 hundred years ago?
   _____

8. Write the years where they belong on the time line.
   • 2010   • 2014   • 2015   • 2017   • 2018

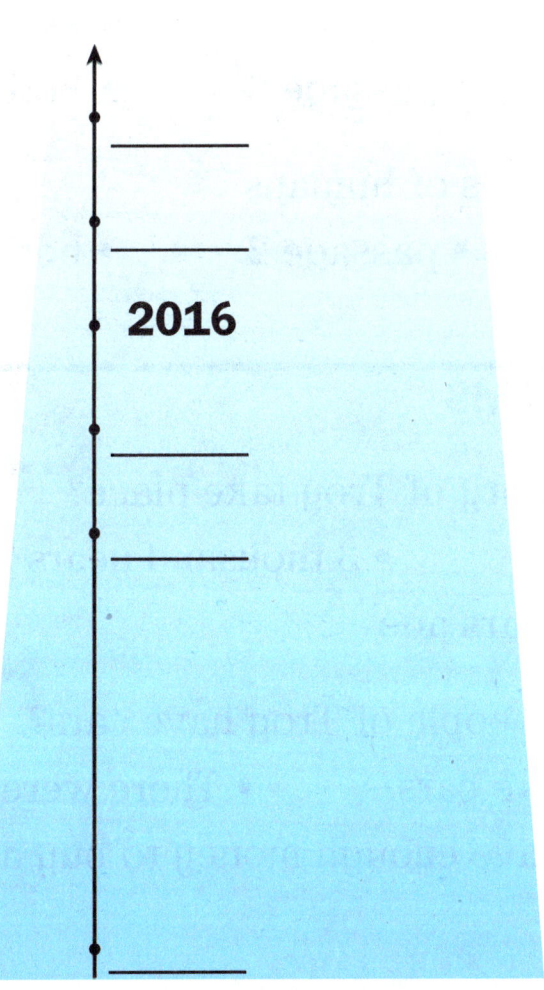

**GO TO PART E IN YOUR TEXTBOOK**

Lesson 64    **65**

# 65  Name _____

## A  INFORMATION ITEMS—Passages 1 and 2

**Compare the passages.**

1. body temperatures
   - passage 1
   - passage 2
   - both passages

2. damage to the human brain
   - passage 1
   - passage 2
   - both passages

3. body temperature of dogs
   - passage 1
   - passage 2
   - both passages

4. fevers
   - passage 1
   - passage 2
   - both passages

5. body temperatures of humans
   - passage 1
   - passage 2
   - both passages

## B  PASSAGE 3 ITEMS

1. When did the story of Troy take place?
   - 300 years ago
   - 3 thousand years ago
   - 1 thousand years ago

2. Why didn't the people of Troy have cars?
   - They didn't like cars.
   - There were no cars yet.
   - They didn't have enough money to buy a car.

3. The people of Troy got in and out of the city through the great _____ .

4. Circle the weapons that soldiers used when they had battles with Troy.
   - swords
   - guns
   - spears
   - tanks
   - planes
   - trucks
   - bows
   - arrows

5. When an army put ladders against the wall of Troy, what did the people of Troy do to the ladders?
   _____

6. When an army dug holes under the wall, what did the people of Troy dump into the holes?
   _____

7. When an army tried to knock down the gate, what did the people of Troy dump on them?
   _____

8. An army could not starve the people of Troy because the people had _____ .

9. Write the years where they belong on the timeline.
   - 1985
   - 1982
   - 1987
   - 1981
   - 1989

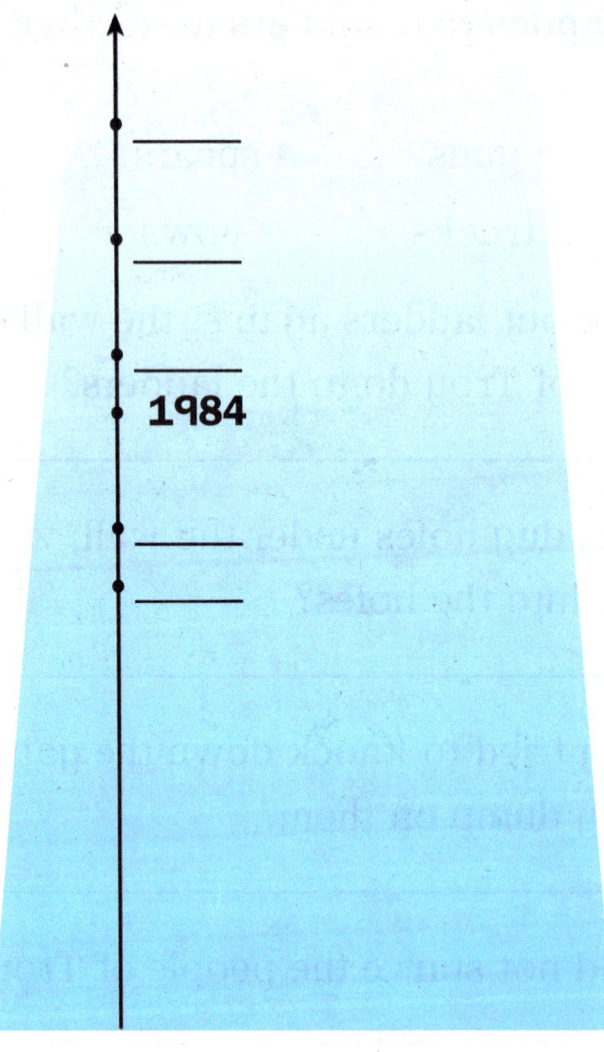

# Name _____  66

## A  INFORMATION ITEMS

Fill in the blanks on the timeline.

1. Write **NOW** next to the dot that shows the year now.
2. Write **3 thousand years ago** next to the right dot.
3. Write **2 thousand years ago** next to the right dot.
4. Write **1 hundred years ago** next to the right dot.
5. Write **1 thousand years ago** next to the right dot.

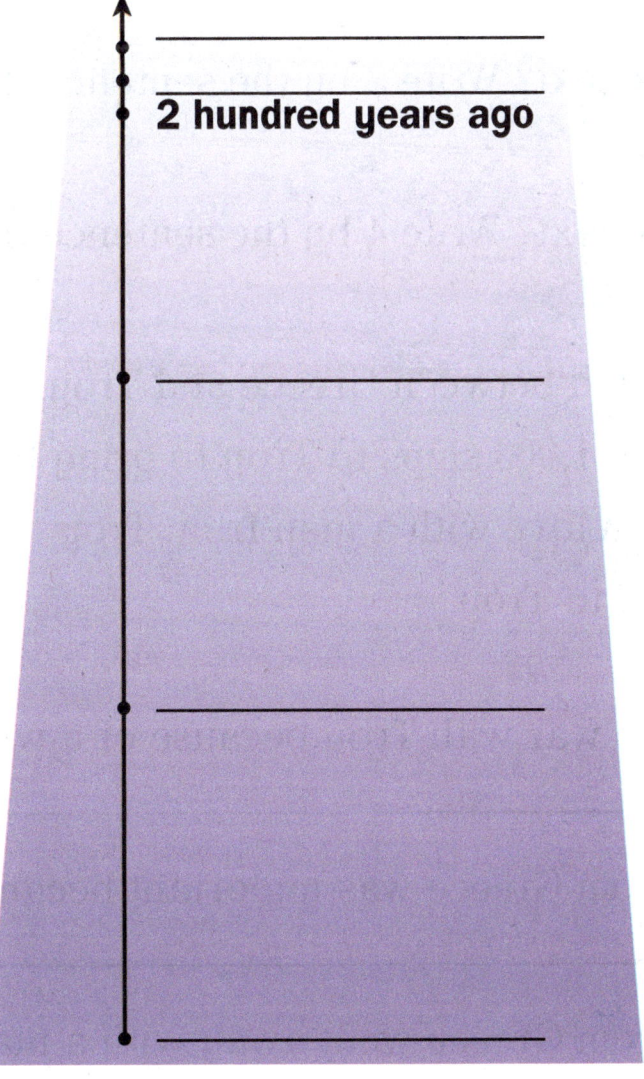

Lesson 66

6. How long ago did the story of Troy take place?

   _____

7. About how long ago did Jesus live?

   _____

## B  STORY ITEMS

1. What happens first? Write 1 by the sentence that tells what happens first.

2. What happens next? Write 2 by the sentence that tells what happens next.

3. What happens next? Write 3 by the sentence that tells what happens next.

4. What happens next? Write 4 by the sentence that tells what happens next.

   ___ A war started between Greece and Troy.
   ___ Greece sent 1,000 ships to Troy to bring back Helen.
   ___ Helen fell in love with a man from Troy.
   ___ Helen went to Troy.

5. Greece went to war with Troy because of a woman named _____.

6. The woman from Greece was important because she was a _____.

7. The woman from Greece went away with a man from _____.

8. How many ships sailed to Troy? _____

9. When the Greek army put ladders against the wall of Troy, what did the people of Troy do? _____

10. When the Greek army dug holes under the wall, what did the people of Troy do? _____

11. When the Greek army tried to knock down the gate, what did the people of Troy do? _____

12. Why couldn't the Greek army starve the people of Troy? _____

13. How long did the war go on? _____

14. If the Greek army got a few men inside the wall of Troy, these men could _____ .

**GO TO PART D IN YOUR TEXTBOOK**

# 67  Name _____

## A  STORY ITEMS

1. For ten years, the army of Greece had the same problem. What was that problem?

    • They couldn't get inside Troy.
    • The soldiers didn't have food.
    • The soldiers kept running away.

    The army of Greece kept using the same four plans to get inside the city.

2. The army put ladders against the _____.

3. The army dug holes under the _____.

4. The army tried to knock down the _____.

5. The army of Greece kept ▓▓▓▓ inside the city.

    • the people of Troy        • arrows and spears
    • boiling water

6. How long did the war between Greece and Troy go on?
   _____

7. What did the Greek army finally build to help solve their problem?
   _____

8. Where did the army put the horse after they finished building it?
   _____

9. What did the people of Troy think the wooden horse was?
    • a cow        • a trick        • a gift

Lesson 67

## B  REVIEW ITEMS

Fill in the blanks on the timeline.

1. Write **now** next to the dot that shows the year now.
2. Write **1 thousand years ago** next to the right dot.
3. Write **3 thousand years ago** next to the right dot.
4. Write **2 hundred years ago** next to the right dot.
5. Write **2 thousand years ago** next to the right dot.

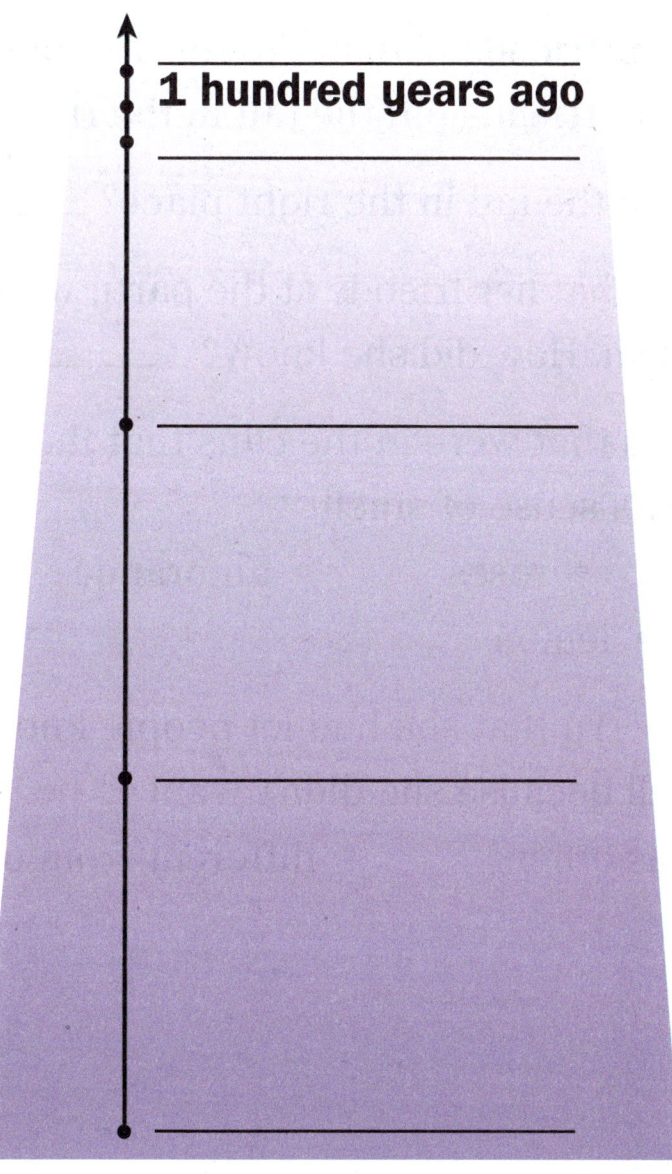

1 hundred years ago

**GO TO PART C IN YOUR TEXTBOOK**

Lesson 67    **73**

## A  STORY ITEMS

1. How old was Bertha? _____

2. What kind of school did Bertha go to? _____

3. Bertha had a super sense of _____.

4. Who had a better sense of smell, Bertha or a hound dog? _____

5. Bertha and her friends played Pin the Tail on the Donkey. Did any of Bertha's friends pin the tail in the right place? _____

6. Did Bertha pin the tail in the right place? _____

7. Bertha knew what her friends at the party were doing without looking at them. How did she know? _____

8. Circle 2 things that were in the cans that the school tester used to test Bertha's sense of smell.
    - pepper
    - roses
    - an orange
    - fish
    - lemon

9. Bertha was sorry that she had let people know about her sense of smell because she didn't want to be ▇▇▇.
    - the same as others
    - different from others
    - others

## B  SKILL ITEM

1. Compare Bertha and a hound dog. Remember, first tell how they're the same. Then tell how they're different.

   _____

   _____

   _____

## C  REVIEW ITEMS

Write **W** for warm-blooded animals and **C** for cold-blooded animals.

1. beetle ___

2. cow ___

3. horse ___

4. spider ___

5. bee ___

6. The temperature inside your body is about _____ degrees when you are healthy.

7. Most fevers don't go over _____ degrees.

The picture shows objects caught in a whirlpool.

8. Write the letter of the object that will go down the whirlpool first. ___

9. Write the letter of the object that will go down the whirlpool next. ___

10. Write the letter of the object that will go down the whirlpool last. ___

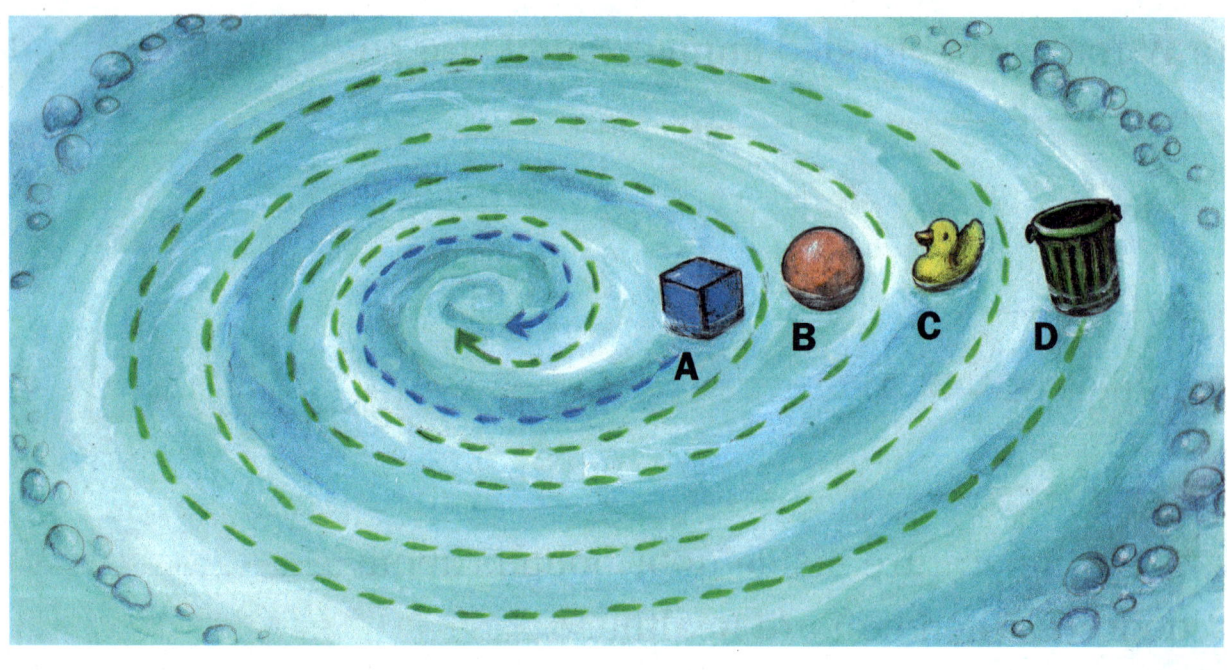

**GO TO PART C IN YOUR TEXTBOOK**

Name _____

**69**

## A  STORY ITEMS

1. Bertha became bored after school got out for the summer. Tell why.
   - She didn't have anything to do.
   - She didn't have a car.
   - She had a fight with her neighbors.

2. What job does Maria Sanchez have?
   - nurse
   - investigator
   - lawyer

3. Had Maria finished her report? _____

4. Where was the oil company supposed to get its water?
   - from deep wells
   - from the creek

5. Where did Maria think the oil company was getting its water?
   - from deep wells
   - from the creek

6. Could Maria prove that what she thought was true? _____

7. How could Bertha help Maria?
   _____

## B  SKILL ITEM

1. Compare Bertha and a regular 15-year-old girl. Remember, first tell how they're the same. Then tell how they're different.
   _____
   _____
   _____

Lesson 69    77

## C  REVIEW ITEMS

Fill in the blanks on the timeline.

1. Write **now** next to the dot that shows the year now.

2. Write **3 thousand years ago** next to the right dot.

3. Write **1 hundred years ago** next to the right dot.

4. Write **2 thousand years ago** next to the right dot.

5. Write **2 hundred years ago** next to the right dot.

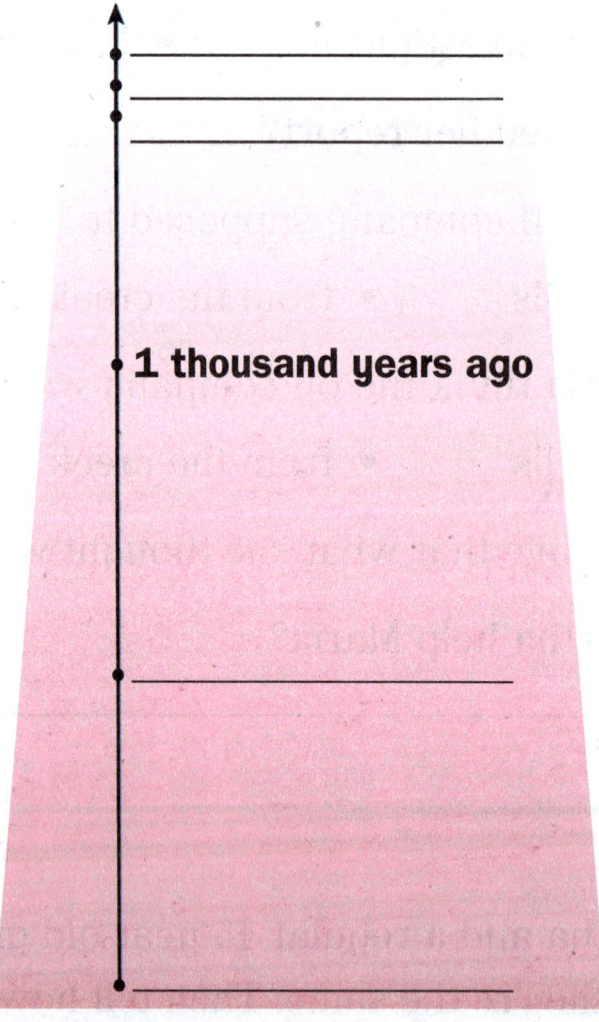

**GO TO PART C IN YOUR TEXTBOOK**

Name _____

**A  SETTING, CHARACTERS, PLOT**

**Answer these questions about the story *Tom's Friend*.**

1. What is the main setting for this story? _____

2. Name the main character in this story. _____

3. Complete the plot for this story. Write the missing words.

   This story is about a little boy named _____ who made friends with a _____ . Tom named his friend _____ . He found the lizard in his _____ . He made a home for his friend out of a _____ tank. Tom discovered that the best home for his friend was in the long grass by the _____ .

**B  STORY ITEMS—*Tom's Friend***

1. What is the message for this story?

   A. Lizards make good house pets.

   B. A fish tank is the best home for a lizard.

   C. A good friend thinks about how their friends feel.

2. Where did Tom find his friend? _____

3. What was his friend? _____

Lesson 70

4. What did he name his friend? _____

5. Why did he give it that name? _____

6. Where did Tom keep his friend? _____

7. Name 3 things he put in his friend's home.
   _____

8. Who showed Tom something he had forgotten to give his friend? _____

9. Name 3 things Bluey couldn't do in the home Tom had for him.
   ① _____
   ② _____
   ③ _____

10. What did Tom decide to do with Bluey at the end of the story?
    _____

## C  SKILL ITEMS

Match the author's purpose to each title. Write **persuade, entertain,** or **explain.**

1. Three Dogs and a Donkey Build a House  _____
2. Choose from 100 Party Ideas  _____
3. Why You Should Get Rid of Your Pets  _____
4. A Joke for Every Day  _____
5. Favorite Tales of the Sea  _____
6. The Pink Tugboat Finds a Friend  _____

**GO TO PART D IN YOUR TEXTBOOK**

Name _____

TEST 4

**1**

Some hairs in the picture are being pushed down. Some are being pulled up. Look at the skin around each hair.

1. Write the letter of each hair that is being pushed down.
   _____

2. Write the letter of each hair that is being pulled up.
   _____

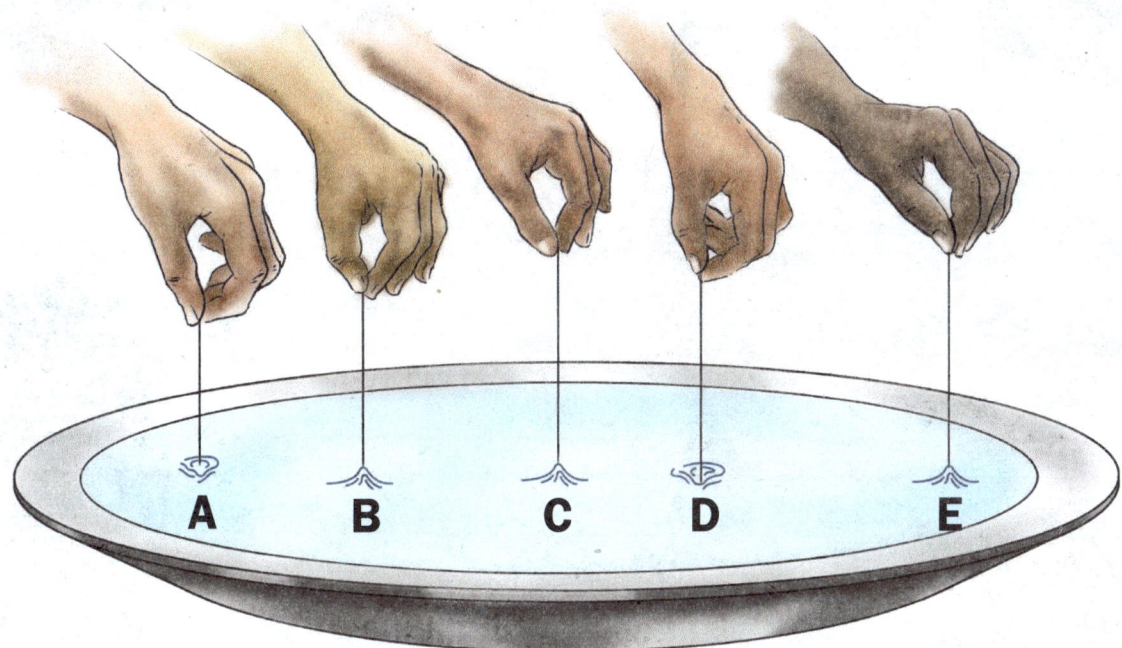

**2**

3. When we weigh very small things, the unit we use is _____ .

Mastery Test 4    81

**3**

4. The food that 3 of the animals eat each day weighs more than those animals. Write the letters of those animals. _____

5. The food that 4 of the animals eat each day does not weigh as much as those animals. Write the letters of those animals.

_____

**4**

6. If you get smaller, your voice gets _____.

7. Tom got smaller. So what do you know about Tom's voice?

_____

8. Write the letter of the ruler that will make the highest sound.
   _____

9. Write the letter of the ruler that will make the lowest sound.
   _____

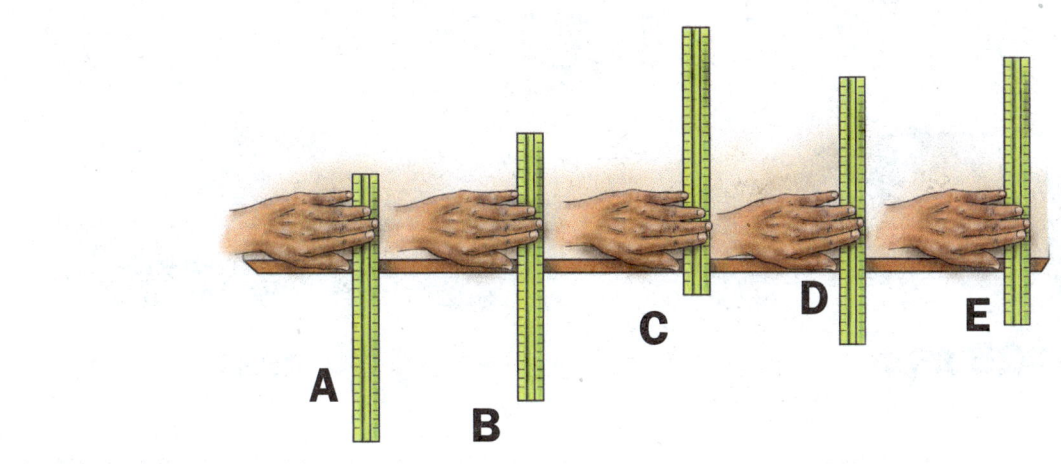

## 5

Each statement tells about how far something goes or how fast something goes. Write **how far** or **how fast** for each item.

10. He ran 5 miles per hour. _____

11. He ran 5 miles. _____

12. The plane was 500 miles from New York City. _____

13. The plane was flying 500 miles per hour. _____

14. When we talk about miles per hour, we tell how _____ something is moving.

## 6

15. When something tries to move in one direction, something else tries to move _____.

Mastery Test 4     83

**TEST 4**

**7**

16. How fast is truck **A** going? _____

17. How fast is truck **B** going? _____

18. Which truck is going faster? _____

**A**  **B**

25 mph          30 mph

**8**

19. How far is it from New York City to San Francisco?
_____

**9  Look at object A and object B.**

20. Write one way that tells how both objects are the same.
_____

21. Write 2 ways that tell how object A is different from object B.
_____

**Object A**          **Object B**

84   Mastery Test 4

## 10 For each item, write the underlined word or words from the sentences in the box.

> The traffic was moving forty miles per hour.
>
> He is supposed to make a decision in a couple of days.

22. What underlining means **two?** _____

23. What underlining means **each?** _____

24. What underlining means **make up his mind?** _____

25. What underlining refers to all the cars and trucks that were moving on the street? _____

26. What underlining means **should?** _____

**END OF TEST 4**

Name _____

TEST 5

**1**

Here's how fast different things can go:

- 20 miles per hour
- 35 miles per hour
- 200 miles per hour
- 500 miles per hour

1. Which speed tells how fast a fast man can run?
   _____

2. Which speed tells how fast a jet can fly?
   _____

3. Which speed tells how fast a fast dog can run?
   _____

**2**

4. When an object gets hotter, the temperature goes _____ .

The arrows show that the temperature is going up on thermometer A and going down on thermometer B.

5. In which picture is the water getting colder, **A** or **B**? _____
6. In which picture is the water getting hotter, **A** or **B**? _____

A    B

Mastery Test 5    87

7. Which letter shows where San Francisco is? _____

8. If you were in San Francisco, which direction would you face if you wanted the wind to blow in your face? _____

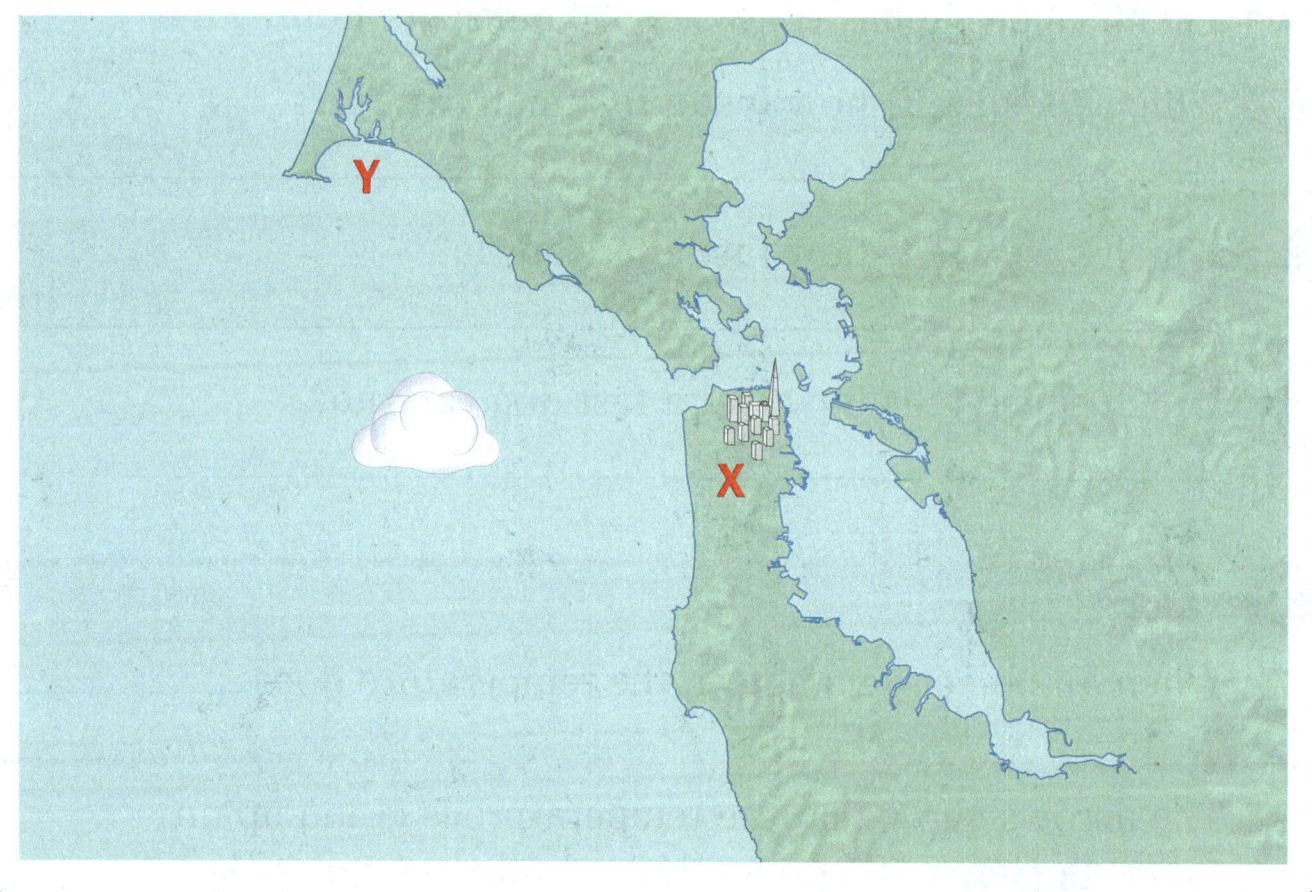

9. When a plane flies from New York City to San Francisco, is it flying in the **same direction** or the **opposite direction** as the wind?

_____

10. Which letter shows where New York City is? _____
11. Which letter shows where San Francisco is? _____
12. Which letter shows where Japan is? _____
13. Which letter shows where the Pacific Ocean is? _____

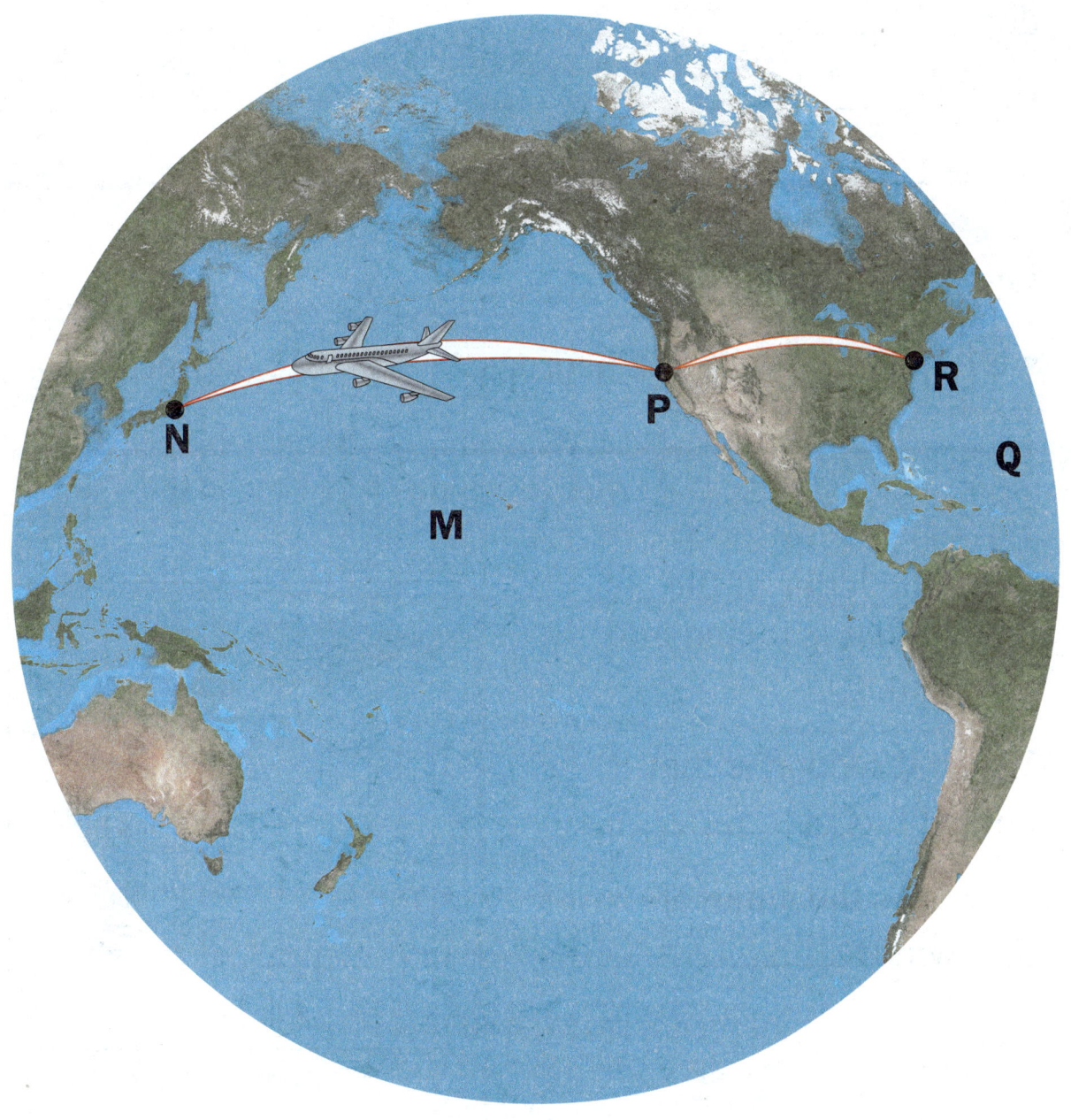

## 5

Write **W** for warm-blooded animals and **C** for cold-blooded animals.

14. beetle ___
15. camel ___
16. spider ___
17. dog ___
18. fly ___

## 6

19. What's the boiling temperature of water?
    - 212 miles
    - 112 degrees
    - 212 degrees

## 7

20. Write the letter of the animal that is facing into the wind. ___

21. Which direction is that animal facing? _____

22. So what's the name of that wind? _____

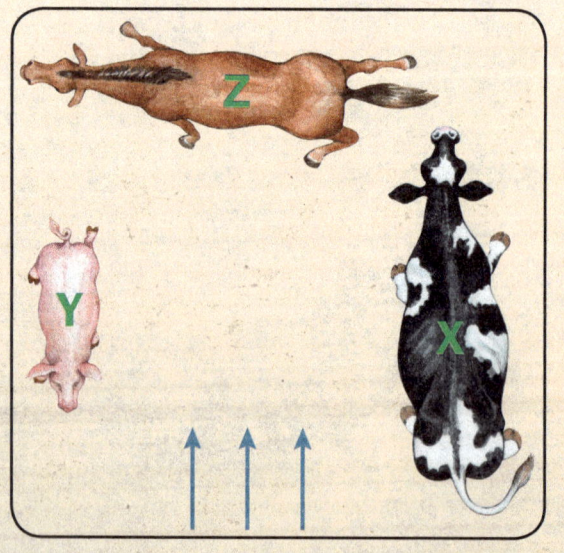

**8**

23. How many states are in the United States? _____

24. The biggest state in the United States is _____ .

25. The second-biggest state in the United States is _____ .

**9**

26. How far is it from San Francisco to Japan?
_____

**10** For each item, write the underlined word from the sentences in the box.

> Several paths continued for a great distance.
> Boiling water will thaw ice in a few moments.
> They were eager to hear the announcement.

27. What underlining means **melt**? _____

28. What underlining means **message**? _____

29. What underlining means **kept on going**? _____

30. What underlining refers to more than two but less than a lot? _____

31. What underlining tells how they felt about hearing the announcement? _____

**11**

Here's a rule: **Every spider has eight legs.**

32. Keb is a spider. So what does the rule tell you about Keb? _____

33. Bop is not a spider. So what does the rule tell you about Bop? _____

**END OF TEST 5**

Name _____

**TEST 6**

**1**

1. Write the letter of each island on the map.
   _____

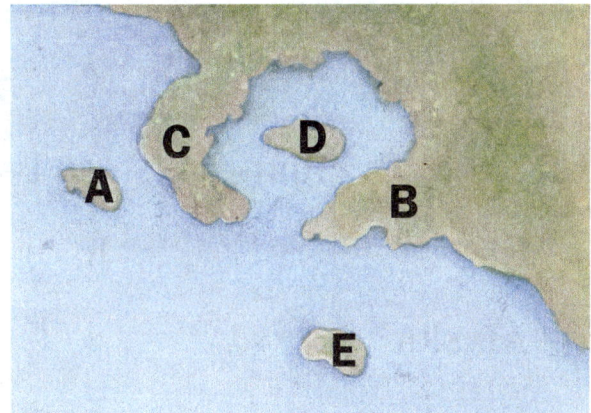

**2**

2. Jar X is filled with fresh water. Jar Y is filled with ocean water. Which jar is heavier? ___

3. Which jar will freeze at 32 degrees? ___

4. Will the other jar freeze when it is **less than** 32 degrees or **more than** 32 degrees?
   _____

Mastery Test 6   93

**TEST 6**

**3**

5. Write the letters of the 9 places that are in the United States.

   _____

   a. Denver           f. Chicago          k. Turkey

   b. Lake Michigan    g. Texas            l. California

   c. China            h. San Francisco    m. Italy

   d. Alaska           i. Ohio

   e. New York City    j. Japan

**4**

6. The ship in the picture is sinking. It is making currents as it sinks. Write the letter of the object that will go down the whirlpool first. ___

7. Write the letter of the object that will go down the whirlpool last. ___

94   Mastery Test 6

8. A plane that flies from Italy to New York City goes in which direction? _____

9. Which letter shows where Italy is? ___

10. Which letter shows where China is? ___

11. Which letter shows where Turkey is? ___

12. Is the United States shown on this map? ___

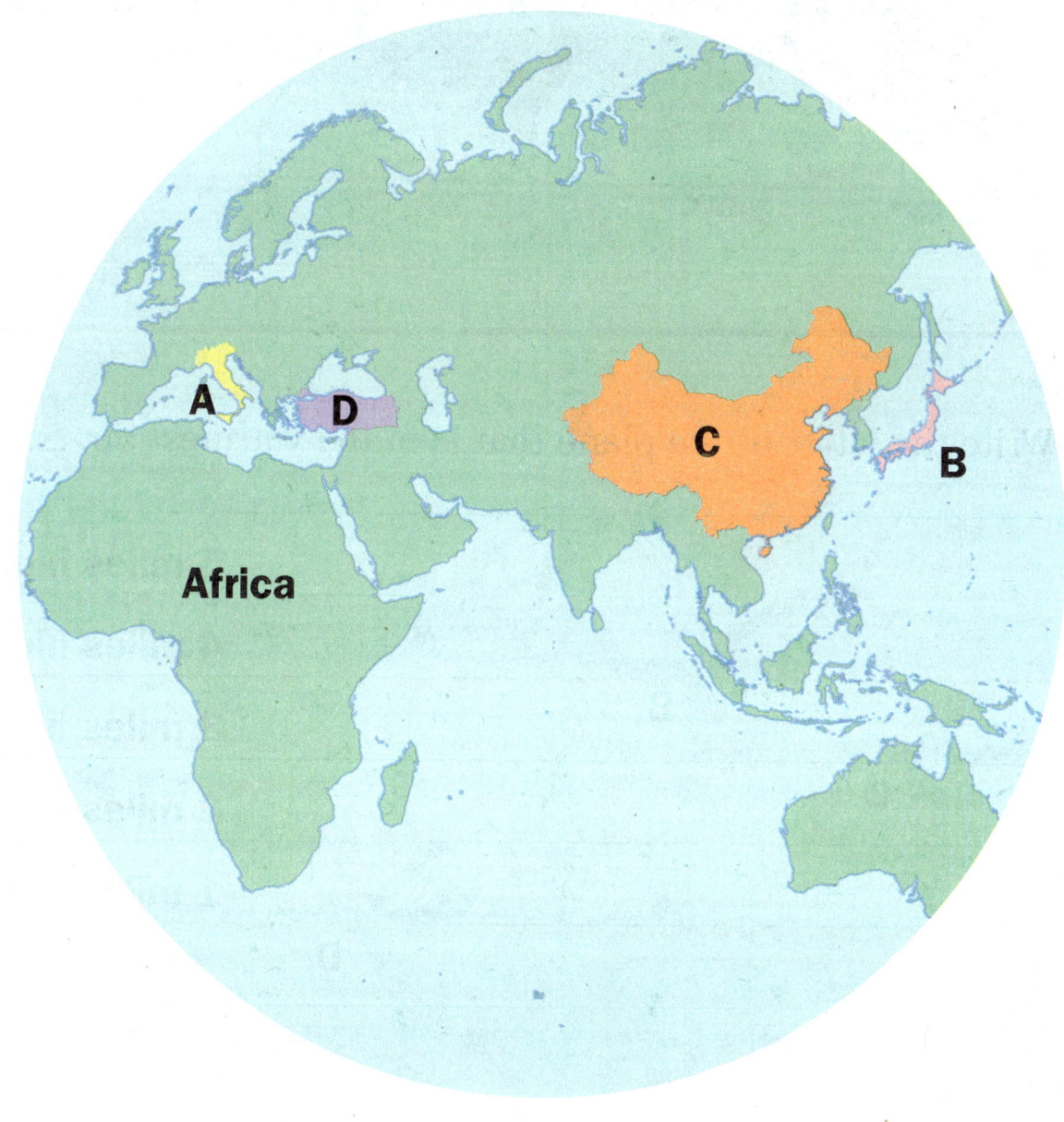

**TEST 6**

**6**

13. Which arrow shows the way Linda's hand will move? ___

14. Which arrow shows the way the crate will move? ___

**7**

15. Write the letter of the plane that is in the warmest air. ___

96  Mastery Test 6

## 8

16. Palm trees cannot live in places that get _____.

17. Name 2 things that grow on different palm trees.
_____

## 9

18. All machines make it easier to for someone to _____.

19. You would have the most power if you pushed against one of the handles. Which handle is that? ___

20. Which handle would give you the least amount of power? ___

## 10

The arrow by the handle shows which way it turns.

21. Which arrow shows the way the log moves? ___

22. Which arrow shows the way the vine moves? ___

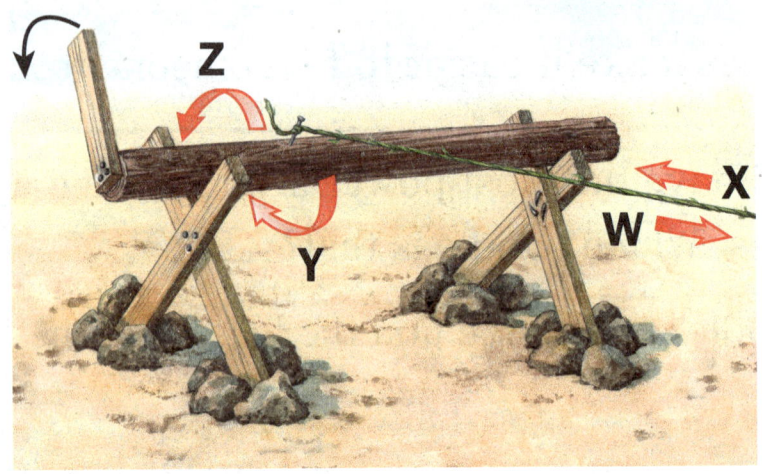

## 11

23. What part does the **G** show? _____

24. What part does the **H** show? _____

25. What part does the **K** show? _____

26. What part does the **J** show? _____

27. Compare object A and object B. First tell how they're the same.
_____

28. Then tell how they're different.
_____

**Object A**  **Object B**

# 13

**For each item, write the underlined word from the sentences in the box.**

> The lifeboat disappeared in the whirlpool.
>
> The smoke swirled in enormous billows.
>
> The occasional foul smell was normal.

29. What underlining names an emergency boat that is on a large ship? _____

30. What underlining means **usual**? _____

31. What underlining names water that goes around and around as it goes down? _____

32. What underlining means **very, very large**? _____

33. What underlining means **once in a while**? _____

**END OF TEST 6**

**TEST 7**

**1**

1. Write the letter of the sun you see early in the morning. ___
2. Write the letter of the sun you see at sunset. ___
3. Write the letter of the sun you see at noon. ___

**2**

4. The temperature inside your body is about _____ degrees when you are healthy.

5. Most fevers don't go over _____ degrees.

**3**

6. Airplanes land at airports. Ships land at _____.

7. Airplanes are pulled by little trucks. Ships are pulled by _____.

8. Airplanes unload at gates. Ships unload at _____.

**4**

9. Which letter shows where Troy used to be? ___
10. Which letter shows where Greece is? ___
11. Which letter shows where Italy is? ___

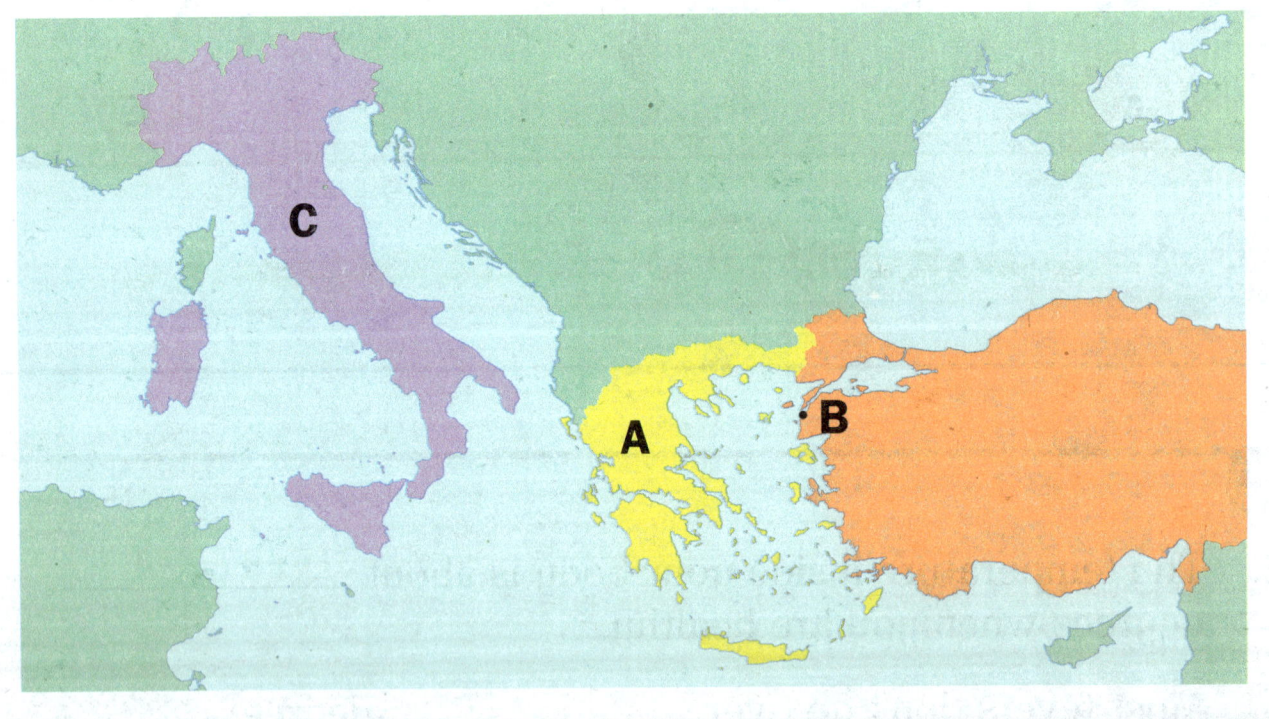

**5**

12. What year is it now? _____

13. In what year did the United States become a country? _____

14. In what year were you born? _____

15. What was the year 1 hundred years ago?
_____

16. What was the year 2 hundred years ago?
_____

17. In what year was the first airplane made? _____

**6**

18. When did the story of Troy take place?
    - 1 thousand years ago
    - 1 hundred years ago
    - 3 thousand years ago

19. Greece went to war with Troy because of a woman named
_____ .

20. The woman from Greece was important because she was a
_____ .

21. The woman from Greece went away with a man from
_____ .

22. How many ships sailed to Troy? _____

23. How long did the war go on? _____

24. If the Greek army could get a few men inside the wall of Troy, those men could _____ .

Mastery Test 7

**TEST 7**

**7**

25. During the war with Troy, what did the Greek army build to help them get inside Troy? _____

26. What was inside this object? _____

27. What did they do after they came out of the object?
    _____

28. Who won the war, Troy or Greece? _____

**8**

29. Compare Linda and Kathy. Remember, first tell how they're the same. Then tell how they're different.
    _____
    _____

> They <u>constructed</u> an <u>enormous</u> <u>machine</u>.
>
> She <u>survived</u> until she was <u>rescued</u>.
>
> The <u>soldiers</u> <u>protected</u> their <u>equipment</u>.

For each item, write the underlined word from the sentences in the box.

30. What word means **saved from danger?**
_____

31. What word means **very large?**
_____

32. What word means **machines and tools?**
_____

33. What word names something that helps people do work?
_____

34. What word means **managed to stay alive?**
_____

35. What word means **built?** _____

36. What word names **men and women in the army?**
_____

**END OF TEST 7**

# Fact Game Scorecard Sheet

## Fact Game for Test 4

| 1  | 2  | 3  | 4  | 5  |
|----|----|----|----|----|
| 6  | 7  | 8  | 9  | 10 |
| 11 | 12 | 13 | 14 | 15 |
| 16 | 17 | 18 | 19 | 20 |

## Fact Game for Test 6

| 1  | 2  | 3  | 4  | 5  |
|----|----|----|----|----|
| 6  | 7  | 8  | 9  | 10 |
| 11 | 12 | 13 | 14 | 15 |
| 16 | 17 | 18 | 19 | 20 |

## Fact Game for Test 5

| 1  | 2  | 3  | 4  | 5  |
|----|----|----|----|----|
| 6  | 7  | 8  | 9  | 10 |
| 11 | 12 | 13 | 14 | 15 |
| 16 | 17 | 18 | 19 | 20 |

## Fact Game for Test 7

| 1  | 2  | 3  | 4  | 5  |
|----|----|----|----|----|
| 6  | 7  | 8  | 9  | 10 |
| 11 | 12 | 13 | 14 | 15 |
| 16 | 17 | 18 | 19 | 20 |

# Thermometer Chart
## for Check 7 through Check 13

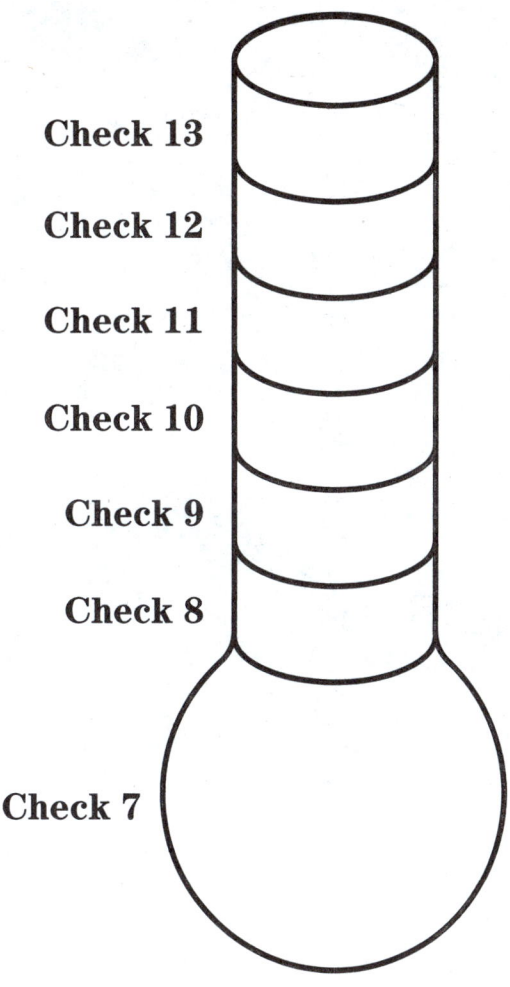

Thermometer Chart **109**